T0359905

Learning to Drive

Drive

the **L** TRENT way

KERRY O'SULLIVAN

with
'Accelerated
Learning'

HarperCollins*Publishers*

First published in Australia in 1988
This revised edition published in 2012
for Trent Driving School Pty Limited
by HarperCollins*Publishers* Australia Pty Limited
ABN 36 009 913 517
harpercollins.com.au

Copyright © Kerry O'Sullivan 2012

The right of Kerry O'Sullivan to be identified as the author of this work has been asserted by him in accordance with the *Copyright Amendment (Moral Rights) Act 2000*.

This work is copyright. Apart from any use as permitted under the *Copyright Act 1968*, no part may be reproduced, copied, scanned, stored in a retrieval system, recorded, or transmitted, in any form or by any means, without the prior written permission of the publisher.

HarperCollins*Publishers*
Level 19, 201 Elizabeth Street, Sydney NSW 2000

ISBN 978 0 6465 7326 7

Cover design by Natasha Cantello
Typeset by Kirby Jones
Printed and bound in China by RR Donnelley on 128gsm Matt Art

8   23

Learning to Drive

Drive

the **L TRENT**
way

KERRY O'SULLIVAN

Contents

Who Is Responsible?

1 Controls

2 Procedures

3 Initial Traffic

4 Secondary Traffic

5 The Open Road

6 Slow-speed Manoeuvring

7 Know the Enemy 116

8 The Complete Driver 119

Who Is Responsible?

The following scenario is continually happening in one form or another within the community.

A teenager wishes to drive. They expect to be able to drive competently and safely. They are instructed one way or another to some degree of basic car control. This instruction could be totally inadequate and incorrect. The learner, who has no knowledge on the subject, accepts it as the requirement, because it is given by a superior, by someone who 'knows'.

The learner does a short test with the licensing authority and is issued with a licence. Why should this new driver doubt their competency?

Yet within a short time, although driving to the best of their ability, this driver is involved in a fatal crash. The law will offer no leniency because of lack of skill. The skills they were presented with were inadequate; they were not told this, they were classified as competent.

How can we as a society say that the instructing persons, the licence evaluator, and the Government (which decrees the standard required) are free from blame. They have not done their best to equip this person for a potentially dangerous task.

Yet we do absolve these people. The total blame is laid with the new driver.

This is unacceptable and this book is the first stage in rectification of this situation.

Introduction

There is a view in the community that driving is divided into two stages. Firstly, there is the initial learning process. Secondly, after licensing, those that are interested take 'defensive' driving courses to rectify their faults.

This is an incorrect view. All the techniques needed in driving should be taught from the initial stages. No method that needs rectification should be used. No technique or habit should be developed without supervised direction. It is infinitely more difficult to change an instilled bad habit than to develop a new one.

Why Have a Driving Technique?

Driving, like sport, is a dexterous activity and those who participate will be of varying standards.

You may take a racquet or a club and teach yourself, with some amateur guidance, to play tennis or golf and reach a certain standard, but those who have been professionally trained and practise a sound technique will be infinitely superior. The same applies to driving.

In sport, when under pressure, professionally instilled, sound techniques win the day.

In driving, when under stress, professionally instilled, sound techniques could save a life.

The Curriculum

This curriculum is divided into six sections, in their correct instruction order. These sections are colour coded to highlight the on-road danger level. They overlap and the transition from one to another is gradual and not apparent. The Manoeuvring section is flexible and may be introduced at any stage from the Procedures section.

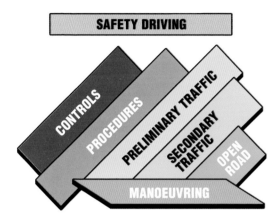

Overriding the whole curriculum are the Safety Driving principles.

The chapters are not lessons. Learning to drive is an individual process and progress will depend on the ability to absorb the tuition. Once a section has been completed, the skills within are continually revised until the curriculum is completed.

Each training session should have a specific purpose. Instructing persons must be limited to those well versed in the curriculum and with knowledge of the progress made in previous sessions.

The new driver is expected to have knowledge of the rules of the road before starting to learn to drive. The practical application of these rules will be encountered during the learning process and the instructing person will clarify any doubts that arise.

Remember that the rules are not there to restrict but to organise the traffic flow for the safety and convenience of all road users. At the end of each section, there is a supplement with rules pertaining to that section.

Your Trent Driver Trainer will supply you with a **Student Record Card** that will record your progress through the learning process.

Safety Driving

At road crashes, we often hear one party or another offer the excuse 'I didn't see them'. Without evaluation, this could be considered glib justification, but the fact is these people are telling the truth. They either did not see the vehicle or only saw it when they were past the point of evasion.

Why didn't they see?

Because they had never been taught the correct use of vision and perception in driving. They didn't possess the correct safety procedures.

This is the purpose of *Safety Driving*: to give a method by which correct vision and the perception from that vision is used to maximum advantage. **To see all and be aware of what is seen, and have a course of action to follow is Safety Driving.**

This is learned through the **Safety Wheel**, a device that links together all the factors needed for safe driving. From this, new drivers recognise potentially dangerous situations and have a course of action to follow. The Safety Wheel is designed to give the learner one set of sequenced safety procedures that can be used in all situations. This will eliminate the need to learn by '**scare experiences**', after licensing, which is the present unsatisfactory method that applies to most new drivers.

The Safety Wheel

There is a natural progression of Safety Factors in Trent's **Safety Wheel** that dictates the driving sequence that is to be followed at all times. Driving decisions are made with the eyes.

How do you 'look' when driving? With three sequential actions! The first of these is **AIM HIGH** – look to the visible end of the road.

The second is **KEEP THE EYES ON THE MOVE** — look for potential trouble.

Third, from these steps we can **SEE THE WHOLE SCENE** — from footpath to footpath to the visible end of the road.

When driving with correct vision a **SAFETY CUSHION** can be established. This is '**our** space'.

With these factors in operation, **EARLY DECISIONS** are made. These lead to us to be predictable to other drivers. If other drivers see you early enough, they will not run into you.

An early decision gives time to **BE SEEN** by other road users. Be Seen, an Early Decision and a Safety Cushion allow us to always **HAVE AN ESCAPE** in our driving.

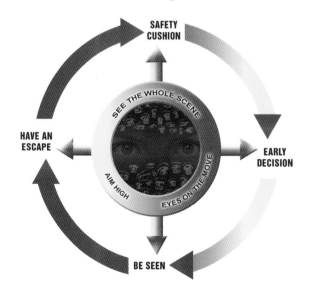

Accelerated Learning

This book is an integral part of the *Trent Accelerated Learning Program*; this whole program is based on this curriculum. With the addition of the Student Record Card, the Lesson Planner, the Student Particulars Form and the services of a fully trained **Trent Driver Trainer**, a student will be introduced to *Accelerated Learning*.

Accelerated Learning is where all the resources of the training and the abilities of the student focus on the training objective. When this happens the time taken to be trained is dramatically reduced – **by at least a factor of seven**. Those that partake in this program will be pleasantly surprised at how easily and quickly they reach the required standard, to not only pass the test but also to be a confident and safe driver, with a minimum of trauma and cost.

1 Controls

Controls Explained

This section is an introduction to the motor vehicle. The controls, both dash and driving, are explained, and **what they are**, **what they do** and **how to use them** are examined in detail.

Over the years the motor vehicle has been refined and its efficiency greatly improved. Much sophisticated gadgetry has been introduced but the basic concept is little different than it was 50 years ago. Dash controls and instrumentation vary considerably from car to car, but the control functions that are essential to driving have remained unchanged and are common to all vehicles.

SEATING POSITION

Firstly, it is important to be a comfortable distance from both the steering wheel and the pedals. Being too close or too far from the controls will reduce your efficiency as a driver. A good guide is for you to be comfortably seated so that with both arms outstretched your wrists will rest on the top of the steering wheel. In most cases your physique will dictate that this is also an adequate distance from the pedals. Some minor adjustment to the seat, seat back or steering wheel may be needed.

SEAT BELTS

No doubt you are familiar with seat belts. Remember it is now your responsibility as a driver to make sure all in the car wear seat belts correctly.

REAR-VISION MIRRORS

The third individual adjustment is to the mirrors. As well as the interior rear-vision mirror, most vehicles have one or more outside mirrors. All rear-vision mirrors need to be adjusted to suit the driver.

The interior mirror, from the normal seating position, will show an equal amount of the surrounds of the rear window. The lower centre of the rear window should appear in the lower centre of the mirror.

Outside mirrors are adjusted so that the side of the vehicle is just visible and an equal amount of the road surface and the scene above is reflected. A glance in the mirrors is all that is required. Your major attention must be on the road ahead.

The mirrors should be checked approximately every 10 seconds. Before any voluntary driving action, check the mirrors to assess the affect of such action on the following traffic.

STEERING WHEEL

The steering wheel is connected to the front wheels. It is used to direct the vehicle by turning in the direction of intended travel. The steering wheel is held by both hands in equal positions, at or above a quarter to three. The thumbs are placed on the inner front of the wheel. The wrists are slightly inwards and the elbows  are down and relaxed. Your grip should be light. If more pressure is required when turning, the effort required will automatically dictate the amount of extra pressure needed.

HORN

The horn is usually positioned on the steering wheel. In well-designed vehicles it may be used without the hands leaving the steering wheel rim. The horn is only used as a warning to others of developing danger.

WINDSCREEN WIPERS

Generally the windscreen wiper controls are located on a steering column arm which can be operated by finger control. Most windscreen wiper controls incorporate a windscreen washer.

SPEEDOMETER

The speedometer is centrally located on the dashboard and is calibrated in kilometres per hour (km/h). While driving, constant checking will enable you to maintain a speed within the prescribed limit.

1 Controls

IGNITION SWITCH

The present trend is for vehicles to have a combination switch, which is operated by a key on the steering column, for the function of steering wheel lock, accessories switch, 'ignition on' position and motor starter. These functions are activated by turning the key clockwise. Turning the key anticlockwise reverses the process.

When the 'ignition on' position is reached all other instruments are activated.

ELECTRICAL WARNING LIGHT

When the motor is running the warning light should be out. If the light is on there is an electrical malfunction in the vehicle. It must be rectified as a matter of urgency.

TEMPERATURE LIGHT

If the temperature warning light comes on while the engine is running, the engine is overheating and must be checked immediately. To continue driving the vehicle will damage the motor.

OIL PRESSURE LIGHT

If the warning light is on while the motor is running, the engine lubrication is not sufficient. An immediate check is necessary or a major breakdown could occur.

TURN INDICATORS

On the side of the steering column is an arm that operates the turn indicators. They are activated by pushing the lever in the direction of intending steering-wheel turn. The indicator arm activates flashing lights at the front and rear of the vehicle, on the side indicated. A light is displayed on the dashboard and a clicking noise is audible while the signals are in operation. These indicators are self-cancelling during the cornering procedure.

At other times they must be manually cancelled. The signals are finger operated, with the hand remaining on the steering wheel.

The signals are used as an indication to others of our intentions. For corners, signal approx. 60 metres before the corner.

On other occasions (leaving the kerb, lane change, etc.) give at least a 4-second warning.

HEADLIGHTS

All vehicles have controls that operate the parking lights, the headlights – in both the low and high beam position – and a headlight flashing switch. It is necessary to be able to operate these and also know when and where high beam may be used. The headlight flashing switch is an integral part of BEING SEEN.

ACCELERATOR

The pedal on the right is the accelerator. It governs the amount of power delivered by the motor. It is the **GO** pedal and is operated by the right foot. It is progressive in operation: the further the pedal is depressed, the more power the motor develops. Keep your heel on the floor while using this pedal.

FOOTBRAKE

The pedal immediately to the left of the accelerator is the footbrake. It is the **STOP** pedal. This works on all four wheels and is operated by the right foot. The brake action is progressive; the more pressure applied the quicker the vehicle will slow or stop. The pedal is depressed until it becomes firm and the amount of pressure applied at this point governs the braking action.

Your right foot function in driving is to operate the accelerator (the go pedal) or the footbrake (the stop pedal).

In both automatic and manual vehicles, the right foot **only** is used for braking.

When the footbrake is applied, the stop lights at the rear of the vehicle are illuminated, warning those travelling behind of your intentions (BEING SEEN).

HANDBRAKE

The handbrake is generally located between the front seats. It operates on the rear wheels only. It is used for locking the rear wheels when leaving the vehicle or when starting if the vehicle will roll in the opposite direction of intended travel. Under normal circumstances it should not be applied when the vehicle is moving. However, in the case of footbrake failure, the handbrake could be applied to stop the vehicle as it operates through an independent system.

To apply the handbrake raise the lever with the left hand until it becomes quite firm. A ratchet locks the brake in this applied position. To release, apply pressure with the thumb to the knob at the end of the lever and lift, which releases the ratchet, then lower the lever to the floor. Some handbrakes are mounted under the dashboard.

GEARS

AUTOMATIC GEARS

Most automatic vehicles have a centrally located lever for use by the left hand.

The gear positions usually are:

PARK	**P**	Used when the car is not in use. It locks the drive wheels. The car is started in Park.
REVERSE	**R**	For backwards operation.
NEUTRAL	**N**	No gear selected. The vehicle can be started in neutral.
DRIVE	**D**	General driving position.
3RD GEAR	**3**	
2ND GEAR	**2**	Gear '**hold**' positions. Selection negates the automatic change mechanism. Used for towing or extended slow-speed driving.
IST GEAR	**I**	

MANUAL GEARS

Most manual gear levers are centrally located on the floor, although occasionally the lever is located on the steering column.

Manual gears are usually in this selection pattern:

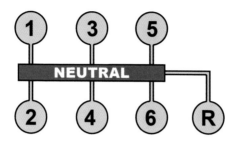

NEUTRAL	No gear selected.
1st GEAR	The starting gear. Under normal operation the vehicle is taken to 20 km/h.*
2nd GEAR	The speed is increased to 40 km/h.*
3rd GEAR ⎫ 4th GEAR ⎭	General driving gears. Used in most city driving.
5th GEAR ⎫ 6th GEAR ⎭	Top gears, where the highest speed for the least engine effort can be achieved.
REVERSE	For backwards operation.

Minimum change points used in the learning stages

However, the engine will not perform efficiently in the high gears if the speed is reduced or the load increased (e.g. by climbing a steep hill).

As the speed **increases**, the gears are changed **up**.

As the speed **decreases** or the load increases, the gears are changed **down**.

CLUTCH

The clutch is a coupling between the motor and the drive wheels. The pedal is operated by the left foot.

When the pedal is depressed the motor is disconnected from the drive wheels.

When the pedal is raised the motor is connected to the drive wheels and the vehicle moves.

(These diagrams are for rear-wheel-drive vehicles, but the same principles apply for front-wheel-drive vehicles.)

Although the motor and the wheels are disengaged when the clutch pedal is depressed, the point of engagement is not when the pedal is fully released but somewhere in between. This point of engagement is called *friction point*.

Before engagement, the disc part of the clutch connected to the motor is spinning very fast, while the disc part connected to the wheels is stationary. If the pedal is raised quickly through friction point these discs come together in a sudden jarring movement and cause stalling or kangaroo hopping. To eliminate this, care is needed at friction point.

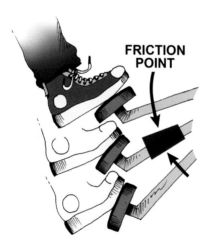

FRICTION POINT

To use the clutch correctly raise the pedal to friction point and hold the pedal still, until the vehicle has moved forward 2 or 3 car lengths, then slowly fully release the pedal.

Friction point occurs when the vehicle starts to move. The key to correct clutch use when starting is not the upward movement of the pedal but the holding action.

*Raise the pedal until the car just begins to move, then **hold** the pedal.*

The clutch is also used to disconnect the motor from the wheels, to enable the gears to be changed. During this operation care must also be taken at friction point, although the higher the gear the easier the clutch operation.

Supplement

PRACTICE ENVIRONMENT
A wide, flat suburban road that has minimum traffic.

CONDITIONS
Preferably daylight and fine weather. Definitely not a wet night.

LAWS AND REGULATIONS
A full knowledge is needed of the laws and regulations relating to:

LEARNER'S LICENCE	When to be carried and produced? The display of L plates? Who may instruct?
LIGHTS	What lights are required at night? When is high beam used?
SIGNALS	What signals must be given? When must they be given?
HORN	When is the horn to be used?
SEAT BELTS	When are seat belts required? Who must wear seat belts?
PERSONS IN VEHICLES	Keeping within the vehicle? Alighting from vehicles?
ALCOHOL	What are the prescribed limits for all drivers? What quantities are required to reach these limits?

DO YOU KNOW?

The average family car weighs over 1,000 kg. The only contact between this mass and the road surface is through the tyres. The contact area for each tyre is only the area of a shoe sole.

This stresses the importance of good quality tyres, properly inflated. It is only their adhesion that enables control to be maintained. Develop the habit of checking the condition of the tyres and the cleanliness of the windows and mirrors.

COMMON FAULTS AND MISCONCEPTIONS

It is thought that because cars are heavy, strength is needed to operate the controls. This is not so. In modern cars all controls, if used correctly, require minimum effort.

It is said that to use the clutch when starting, the pedal should be raised slowly. This is incorrect – holding at friction point is the key to correct starting.

ABILITY REQUIREMENTS
Do you know:

	YES	NO
Your correct seating position and mirror adjustments?	❑	❑
The position and function of all dash controls and gauges? Can you use these controls?	❑	❑
The position and function of all driving controls?	❑	❑
The points of the Safety Wheel and its purpose?	❑	❑

Use of Controls

N.B. The instructing person is responsible for all traffic situations, driving instructions and control use directions during practice for this section.

This section introduces the use of the driving controls. Vision is examined and the hub of the Safety Wheel is explained in detail. Construction of a Safety Cushion is commenced.

Starting and Stopping

Use of the accelerator, clutch and footbrake.

AUTOMATIC VEHICLES

1. Footbrake on
2. Select Park
3. Start the motor
4. Select Drive
5. Apply the accelerator until an approx. speed of 15 km/h is reached
6. Apply the footbrake and gradually stop the vehicle

N.B. The right foot **only** is to be used on the pedals in automatic vehicles.

MANUAL VEHICLES

1. Clutch in – select neutral
2. Start the motor
3. Select 1st gear
4. Apply the accelerator
5. Raise the clutch to friction point and hold until the vehicle has travelled 3 car lengths, then release
6. Accelerate to 15 km/h
7. Clutch in and gradually stop the vehicle with the footbrake

When stopping, reduce pressure on the footbrake just before the vehicle comes to a standstill. This will eliminate a jarring stop.

Repeat these procedures 5 or 6 times and some initial feel for the pedals will develop.

Steering

There are two recommended methods of steering: **pull push** and **hand over hand**.

PULL PUSH STEERING

With pull push steering, on right turns, the process is initiated by a pulling action of the right hand. As the lowering right hand turns the wheel the left hand slides down the wheel. When the right hand reaches 5 o'clock the left hand grips the wheel at 7 o'clock and pushes upwards to 11 o'clock. At the same time the right hand slides up the wheel. This process is repeated until the wheel is turned sufficiently.

On left turns the process is the same except that the pulling left hand initiates the turn.

When exiting from corners, forward momentum tends to return the front wheels to the straight-ahead position. Wheel return speed depends on the amount of acceleration applied and at times can be rapid. If the speed of the steering wheel return is excessive, use pressure with the palm of the hands to slow it down. A reduced pull push hand action should be used in conjunction with the steering wheel return.

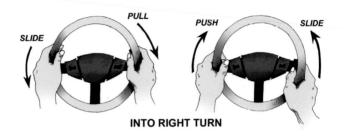

INTO RIGHT TURN

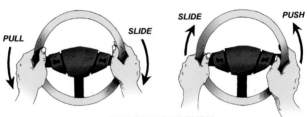

OUT OF RIGHT TURN

INTO LEFT TURN

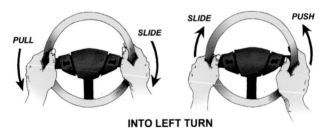

OUT OF LEFT TURN

If, after turning, the straightening up process needs assistance, the first action is to pull down with the hand opposite to the one that initiated the turn.

So for right turns the pulling right hand initiates the turn and the pulling left hand initiates the wheel return. For left turns the pulling left hand initiates the turn and the pulling right hand initiates the wheel return.

In this method of steering, the hands never cross or enter the top or bottom 10 centimetres of the steering wheel arc.

HAND OVER HAND STEERING

With hand over hand steering, for right turns, before the turn, the left hand is moving to 10 o'clock. The next action is to take the steering wheel over to the right with the left hand. As the left hand moves towards 4 o'clock the right hand goes over the left, to 12 o'clock and pulls the wheel downwards to 4 o'clock. The left hand returns to 10 o'clock to repeat the process.

For left turns the opposite applies. The first action is to place the right hand at 2 o'clock and initiate the process.

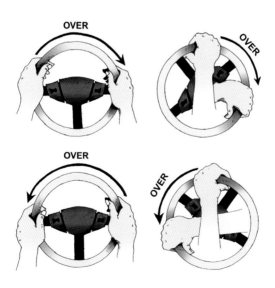

The right turn action is between 10 o'clock and 4 o'clock. The left turn action is anticlockwise between 2 o'clock and 8 o'clock.

The hand over hand action is continuous, with both hands operating as though lifting a weight on a rope.

Hand over hand steering is only used into corners, never out of corners, or palm pressure could not be applied in the automatic steering wheel return process. The action out of corners for hand over hand steering is the same as for pull push steering.

So, in hand over hand steering, for left turns the right hand initiates the turn and the pulling right hand initiates the wheel return process. For right turns the left hand initiates the turn and the pulling left hand initiates the wheel return process.

Hand over hand steering has its limitations and is only used on corners that under normal driving circumstances would be taken under 40 km/h. It is mostly used on right-angle corners as found in built-up areas. If you use hand over hand steering, knowledge of and the ability to use pull push steering is also needed. Pull push steering is used on faster bends and on the open road.

OVER-STEERING

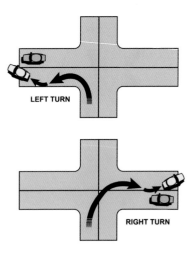

LEFT TURN

RIGHT TURN

Over-steering can occur on exiting from corners. On left turns over-steering heads the vehicle towards the kerb; on right turns over-steering heads the vehicle towards oncoming traffic. Over-steering is very dangerous and any trace must be eliminated.

There are two reasons for over-steering: Firstly, the vehicle is driven past the correct turning point so that the steering wheel must be turned very quickly to complete the turn. This causes an over-steering exit from the corner.

Secondly, the vehicle on exiting from the corner is allowed to point directly down the road before the straightening up process is commenced. Consequently during straightening up the vehicle heads into an over-steering exit.

A good technique for steering cannot be over-emphasised. In a quick-reaction, pressure situation it could save your life.

Once a method of steering has been developed it must be continually practised. In these early stages it is integrated with starting, accelerating, slowing and stopping practice. Numerous left and right turns are needed.

Vision

During this practice period an explanation of vision is needed to ensure that correct seeing habits are instilled.

The eyes are hemispherical, which allows a 180° range of vision.

This range is divided into **central** vision and **peripheral** vision.

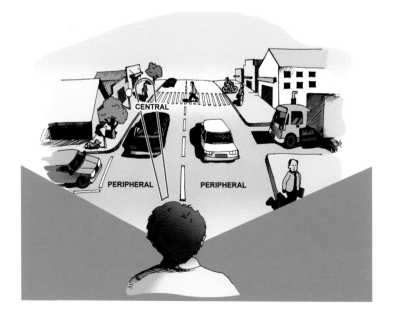

Central vision is our sharp focus. It is the point of immediate attention and the area of utmost clarity. We read with central vision. The area covered by central vision is small.

When central vision is concentrated on an object, the area around is visible but in a blurred fashion. This blurred area is *peripheral vision* or fringe vision. Peripheral vision acts as an attention getter for central vision. The normal process of vision is therefore from fringe to central in a continuous scanning process. The eyes on average transmit 30 to 40 pictures per second to the mind. From this we can see that the eye is capable of doing any job demanded of it. It is the awareness and perception of what we see that is important in driving.

As the vehicle moves the picture changes every split second, demanding that our eyes stay with the change. Trouble starts when correct vision stops while the vehicle is still moving.

AIM HIGH

During the practice of this section we shall examine AIM HIGH, the first of our three vision procedures.

AIM HIGH means looking well beyond the immediate road surface and surrounding traffic. In fact, look up the road as far as possible.

AIMING HIGH also gives direction for straight steering. You may have a tendency to let your vision drop to the road surface in front of the vehicle, which if repeated could become habit. Steering wander is caused by this short vision.

AIM HIGH is essential to SEEING THE WHOLE SCENE.

The use of vision while walking is a good example of how vision should be used when driving. Natural vision tendencies are displayed here.

When walking, vision is usually projected 40–50 metres ahead, even though walking speed is less than 6 km/h. Yet some people drive at 60 km/h with approximately the same forward vision. These people let the **car lead their eyes**, a very dangerous practice.

Integrate AIM HIGH into your steering practice and then we will examine how to SEE THE WHOLE SCENE and keep the EYES ON THE MOVE.

SEE THE WHOLE SCENE

SEEING THE WHOLE SCENE in driving is getting the '**big picture**'. It is seeing with the whole scope of peripheral vision and central vision from footpath to footpath and to the visible end of the road. The whole scene also includes vision to the rear.

What should be in the whole scene?

The whole scene includes the roadway and its environment. It contains collidable objects: parked cars, trees, animals, light poles, etc., but most importantly it contains people: people on foot, on bikes and in vehicles. People who can walk, drive or ride into your path.

When the car is moving, a minimum vision lead of 10 seconds is required. This means that vision must be to the point where the car will be in 10 seconds.

The view of the big picture is altered by speed. Increased speed demands an increased depth of vision but consequently reduces perception of objects that are close. If we need to be aware of close objects speed must be reduced. Varying speed to suit the needs of vision and perception is essential to SEEING THE WHOLE SCENE.

EYES ON THE MOVE

To see the whole scene and get the big picture the eyes must be kept ON THE MOVE. The big picture is a moving picture and is constantly changing. The eyes must be moving to stay with the picture. Poor drivers let people or situations take all of their attention. Their central vision is pin-pointed on one object and the messages from peripheral vision are ignored.

Why do we keep our eyes on the move?

Because we are looking for potential trouble. If anything is missed we leave a hole in our defences.

Now that we have explained these vision habits, try to apply them in your driving. As the curriculum unfolds, you will find these points examined in more detail.

The Safety Cushion

Let's now consider another section of the Safety Wheel.

The **SAFETY CUSHION** is a clear space maintained right around the vehicle, to give reaction, manoeuvring or stopping room in any situation and at any speed. The safety cushion is our territory and we should stringently guard against others entering it.

The safety cushion is variable and will alter with speed and traffic conditions. More space is needed between cars at 100 km/h than at 20 km/h, so the safety cushion increases with speed. If more space is not available speed is reduced to suit the space that exists.

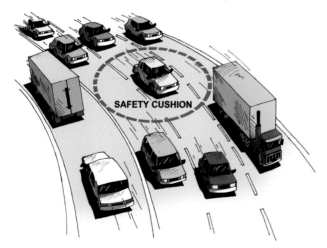

BASIC RULE: Space reduced – Speed reduced
Space increased – Speed increased

At this stage concentrate on developing a side safety cushion (when passing parked cars leave at least 2 metres, if possible) and speed reduction when the safety cushion is reduced (when passing oncoming vehicles in narrow streets, for example).

These functions have all been practised at low speed, with the emphasis on starting, steering, stopping and the initial use of vision.

It is now time to increase speed. Longer stretches of straight road can be covered and an appreciation of acceleration and higher speed braking developed. On manual cars the technique of gear changing is introduced.

(Prior to this, gear changing should be performed by the instructing person with the new driver operating the clutch only.)

Gear Changing

Gear changing is divided into three sections: use of hands, tempo, and use of feet.

USE OF HANDS

The left hand should be comfortably placed on the gear knob. The position can vary from person to person.

Most difficulty is experienced in changes across neutral (e.g. 2nd to 3rd or 4th to 5th). Consequently the palm of the hand beside the knob is recommended for **up** changes across neutral and the reverse palm for **down** changes across neutral (5th to 4th or 3rd to 2nd).

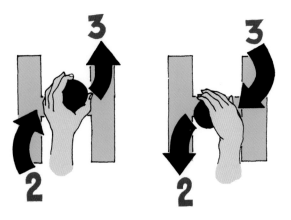

There are no hard and fast rules for hand position in gear changing. If it is comfortable and works successfully it is acceptable.

TEMPO

The correct tempo in gear changing is important as it reduces excessive wear in the gearbox. There should be a pause in neutral between gears. When changing, say the change (i.e. 'one and two', 'four and three', etc.) and pause when you say 'and'. In this way, a correct tempo can quickly be established.

USE OF FEET

The sequence of pedal operation for up changes is:

1. Clutch in
2. Accelerator off
3. Change gear
4. Accelerator on
5. Clutch up

At first, gear changes will be slow, with a tendency towards over revving. These will disappear with practice. The most important factors to achieve are correct sequence and smoothness in changing.

For down changes the pedal sequence is the same, except under some circumstances (e.g. getting ready to move forward) the accelerator is not applied. If slowing, the footbrake is applied and kept on during the change.

Gear changes should be practised on a straight road. A slight hill in the practice area is advisable. Gears are to be changed up and down frequently and speed is to be varied to suit the selected gear. Some down changes must be practised while the vehicle is slowed with the footbrake.

A degree of competence in and understanding of control use and vision habits is needed before the next section is attempted. Mirror use will be introduced; consequently knowledge of blind spots is needed.

Blind Spots

Blind spots exist to the immediate rear and both sides of the car. Side blind spots are not eliminated by mirrors. Outside mirrors move the blind spot further from the side of the vehicle. There are also front blind spots created by the windscreen pillars. Moving forward in the seat eliminates these.

Blind spots can be demonstrated by driving very slowly beside a parked vehicle and seeing the difference between mirror vision and reality. When driving, rear blind spots are checked by a quick glance over the shoulder.

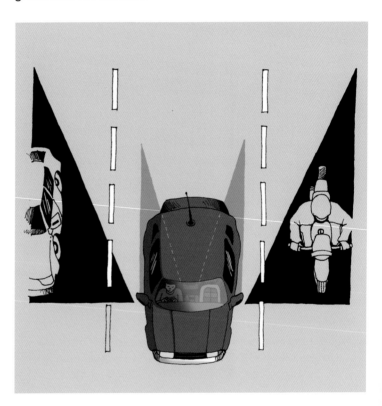

Supplement

PRACTICE ENVIRONMENT
Level suburban blocks with left and right turns and a minimum of traffic.

CONDITIONS
Preferably daylight and fine weather. Definitely not a wet night.

LAWS AND REGULATIONS
A full knowledge is needed of the laws relating to:

KEEP LEFT   What is the basic rule?

SPEED LIMITS   What are they in street light areas?
What is the general limit?
How else is speed restricted?

GIVE WAY   At uncontrolled intersections?
At T-junctions?

ROAD SIGNS   What must you do at a stop sign?
What must you do at a give way sign?

DO YOU KNOW?
The forward movement of the car creates momentum (forward moving energy). This energy increases to the square of speed. If the speed doubles the momentum increases 4 times. This momentum also applies to the occupants. It is the momentum of the occupants, when the vehicle stops in a collision, that causes injury.

COMMON FAULTS AND MISCONCEPTIONS

STEERING FAULTS:
- Hand through the steering wheel. This can interfere with the automatic wheel straightening process.
- Wandering. Check grip pressure – is vision directed to the road just in front of the vehicle?

VISION FAULTS:
It is easy at this stage to develop short vision habits because there is a tendency to direct vision to the road surface immediately in front of the vehicle, particularly when turning. To eliminate this, practise AIMING HIGH.

LEFT FOOT BRAKING IN AUTOMATIC VEHICLES:
There are reasons put forward why this is an acceptable practice. The reasons why it is not are infinitely superior. They are:

- Some left-foot brake users rest the foot on the pedal. The stop lights are continually on, deceiving other drivers.
- When drivers who learn with this method are introduced to manual vehicles, they are disadvantaged when the brake is needed. Their first instinct is to depress the clutch. Valuable safety time is lost.
- In an emergency, when severe braking or manoeuvring is used, momentum and/or centrifugal force will act on the driver. To resist these forces bracing is needed. This must either be with the hands or the feet: the hands cannot be used because they need to be flexible for steering. This leaves the feet. If both feet are positioned over the pedals, the forces will dictate that one or both pedals will be severely depressed, irrespective of the intentions of the driver. The left foot should be placed squarely on the floor to act as a brace against these forces; the right foot must be free to operate the appropriate pedal.

CLUTCH COASTING:

Clutch coasting (driving with the clutch pedal depressed) is caused by incorrect gear change tuition. If only up changes and stops are practised, the accelerator will always be applied before the clutch is raised. The clutch will always be depressed when the brake is applied.

These become conditioned reflexes. This person cannot raise the clutch when the brake is applied and the drive wheels are not engaged. This is dangerous at high speed.

To eliminate clutch coasting, make sure that during gear change practice some down changes are made while braking.

ABILITY REQUIREMENTS
Do you have:

	YES	NO
An ability to move from stationary and then stop?	☐	☐
An ability to steer a straight line and turn the vehicle left and right with a correct steering method?	☐	☐
A knowledge of vision?	☐	☐
An understanding of the three vision habits?	☐	☐
A basic understanding of the SAFETY CUSHION?	☐	☐
An ability to change up and down in the gears?	☐	☐
An awareness of the blind spots?	☐	☐

2 Procedures

The learning process can only be completed by the required amount of repetition. Set procedures allow organised repetition and simplify learning.

Up to this point most attention has been on the use of the controls inside the vehicle. Happenings outside have been the instructing person's responsibility. During this section responsibility for outside happenings will gradually be transferred to the new driver.

Before the procedures are introduced, the other three points of the Safety Wheel are explained. They are EARLY DECISION, BE SEEN and HAVE AN ESCAPE.

N.B. The instructing person is responsible for all traffic situations, driving instructions and control use directions during practice for this section.

Early Decision

The reason that we AIM HIGH and SEE THE WHOLE SCENE is to have time to make judgments and movements without rush or haste. To do this an early decision must be made.

- From an early decision movements can be slow and predictable. An early decision allows stopping to be commenced early and be executed smoothly.
- It allows sufficient time to alter course if needed.
- It makes us predictable to other drivers and allows a safety cushion to be maintained.

If vision is used correctly and a safety cushion maintained, an early decision becomes automatic. Any late decisions indicate a breakdown of vision habits.

There are two types of decisions: **voluntary** and **influenced**.

VOLUNTARY DECISIONS

Voluntary decisions are any legal driving decisions that are made because of the path chosen to reach a certain destination:

- Due to normal happenings in the traffic (stopping, starting, turning, etc.).
- By following the correct procedure at official traffic regulators (traffic lights, stop signs, etc.).

INFLUENCED DECISIONS

Influenced decisions are those made because of the possibility or probability of an outside influence unexpectedly disrupting our driving actions. Most influenced decisions are caused by the probability or actuality of another driver breaking the traffic laws or pedestrians or animals making unexpected movements into our path.

Be Seen

Once an early decision is made it is essential to BE SEEN.

When driving you may be aware of the whole scene and see every possible difficulty, but are all other drivers doing the same? Of course not; how often is it heard at the scene of a collision 'I didn't see him' or 'He came from nowhere'? To reduce the likelihood of a collision other drivers must be aware of your presence.

To make others aware of our presence is an important factor in Safety Driving. Remember vehicles don't cause crashes, it is the drivers. If other drivers are aware of our vehicle they will not knowingly collide with us.

- The primary method of BE SEEN is by the use of signals, either stop or turn. They let others know our actions.
- Make movements early and smoothly so that our actions can be predicted by others.
- If the situation warrants, tap the horn, flash the headlights.
- Do not drive in the blind spots of other vehicles.
- Be wary of large vehicles or objects obstructing your view and the view of you by others.

Never drive where you can't see or be seen.

How do you know if you can be seen? By making eye contact with other drivers! Watch drivers not cars.

Have an Escape

Always try to have an '**out**' in any driving situation. Be prepared for the unexpected. A good SAFETY CUSHION, an EARLY DECISION and BEING SEEN are all ESCAPES.

- Don't use the lane where traffic is entering or merging.
- When stopping in traffic, is there an escape on the left side?
- Examine road shoulders – they may be needed.
- Be in the right gear; if needed use the accelerator to escape.
- When slowing, adjust your braking speed to the actions of the following vehicle.
- When approaching intersections, reduce speed. If a vehicle unexpectedly enters, can you stop?

These points of the Safety Wheel will become more relevant as driving procedures are developed.

Leaving the Kerb

(Level ground)

AUTOMATIC VEHICLES

1. Adjust seat, seat belt and mirrors
2. Check that the handbrake is fully applied
3. Select Park position
4. Start the motor
5. Footbrake on – select Drive
6. Use mirrors to check to the rear (SEE WHOLE SCENE)
7. Indicate (BE SEEN)
8. Release handbrake
9. Check blind spot (SEE WHOLE SCENE)
10. Accelerate to leave the kerb

MANUAL VEHICLES

1. Adjust the seat, seat belt and mirrors
2. Check that the handbrake is fully applied
3. Depress the clutch – gear lever to neutral
4. Start the motor
5. Depress the clutch – select 1st gear
6. Use mirrors to check to the rear (SEE WHOLE SCENE)
7. Indicate (BE SEEN)
8. Accelerate gently – clutch to friction point
9. Release handbrake (at friction point)
10. Check blind spot (SEE WHOLE SCENE)
11. Move from the kerb

Returning to Kerb

AUTOMATIC VEHICLES

1. Check mirrors (SEE WHOLE SCENE)
2. Indicate (BE SEEN)
3. Apply footbrake – approach kerb*
4. Stop close and parallel (keep footbrake applied)
5. Handbrake on
6. Select Park position
7. Ignition off – release footbrake

MANUAL VEHICLES

1. Check mirrors (SEE WHOLE SCENE)
2. Indicate (BE SEEN)
3. Apply footbrake – approach kerb*
4. When under 15 km/h depress clutch
5. Stop close and parallel – keep both feet depressed
6. Handbrake on
7. Select neutral
8. Ignition off
9. Select 1st gear. (If the handbrake is not fully applied this will prevent the vehicle from rolling.)

When stopping in manual vehicles the footbrake is applied before the clutch, except when the speed is under 15 km/h.

*The correct distance should be approximately 20–40 centimetres.

Slow Moving Forward

The ability to slowly move the vehicle forward a short distance and stop is needed in slow-moving traffic, moving forward at lights and in some manoeuvring situations.

AUTOMATIC VEHICLES

In automatic vehicles a delicacy of touch on both accelerator and footbrake is needed. Practise very slow starts and smooth stops from slow speed.

Practise slowly driving over a speed bump and have the vehicle pause at the top and slowly roll down the bump to a stop.

MANUAL VEHICLES

1. Normal amount of accelerator
2. Normal clutch use
3. Once the car moves, depress the clutch *before* releasing the accelerator
4. Gently apply the footbrake

The tendency in these situations is either to attempt to move forward with a minimum of acceleration, causing stalling, or, once moving, to apply the brake before the clutch is depressed, which will also cause stalling.

2 Procedures

Uphill Starts

Prior to this procedure, it has been the responsibility of the instructing person to operate the handbrake on hill starts. If the handbrake is on the right, this procedure can be explained earlier, but remember a certain proficiency in pedal use is needed. Too early an introduction may present difficulties.

AUTOMATIC VEHICLES

The vehicle is to be stopped on a hill sufficiently steep to induce roll back when in Drive. The procedure is:

1. Footbrake on – apply handbrake
2. Apply sufficient acceleration to eliminate roll-back
3. Release handbrake (vehicle to remain stationary)
4. Increase acceleration and move forward

MANUAL VEHICLES

The hill selected need not be particularly steep. The procedure is:

1. Footbrake on – clutch in – select 1st gear
2. Apply handbrake (hold in the released position)
3. Footbrake off – accelerator on (slightly more than normal)
4. Clutch to friction point and pause (this point can be recognised by a change in engine pitch due to the load applied)
5. Handbrake released (vehicle to remain stationary)
6. Increase acceleration and slightly raise clutch and hold for 2 car lengths. The vehicle will move forward

On steep hills more accelerator is needed.

Handbrake starts are **only** used when the vehicle will roll against the direction of intended travel. As proficiency increases, the use of the handbrake on hills will diminish.

This procedure is an exercise in car control. The vehicle is **not** to roll backwards.

Excessive initial acceleration in automatics or raising the clutch too far in manuals will cause the vehicle to move forward when the handbrake is released and control will be lost. The vehicle should only move forward when the accelerator is depressed after the handbrake is released.

Downhill Starts

On downhill starts the handbrake is **not** used.

AUTOMATIC VEHICLES
1. Apply footbrake
2. Release handbrake
3. Release footbrake (vehicle will roll)
4. Apply accelerator

MANUAL VEHICLES
1. Apply footbrake
2. Clutch in – select 1st gear
3. Release handbrake
4. Release footbrake (vehicle will roll) – apply accelerator
5. Clutch up gently

On steep down gradients manual vehicles may be started in 2nd gear.

U-turns

U-turns are used to cause the vehicle to face the opposite direction. A wide flat road with good visibility is needed.

1. Pull in to left kerb
2. Check for traffic – right signal on
3. Use 'slow moving forward' vehicle control
4. When moving turn the steering wheel to full right lock
5. Complete turn

N.B. There is NO right of way when performing a U-turn.

These procedures are integrated into starting, stopping, steering and gear change practice. Two or three repeats at any one time is sufficient.

2 Procedures

Have an Escape at Intersections

HAVE AN ESCAPE governs our speed at intersections. All cross-road intersections, whether governed by lights or signs, should be approached at a speed so that we can stop if the unexpected happens, **irrespective of the right of way**.

When approaching an intersection reduce speed, by accelerator reduction or braking, so that a clear view to both right and left can be obtained, **before** entering the intersection. If speed is not reduced, an escape has not been left. The speed at the intersection is governed by visibility. The vision checks to right and left are made and the **point of decision** reached before entering the intersection.

The **point of decision** is the moment when the possibility of any collision has been eliminated. At the point of decision the accelerator can be applied.

The point of decision varies from intersection to intersection and is governed by the approach speed and the sight distance (how much vision you have into the intersection).

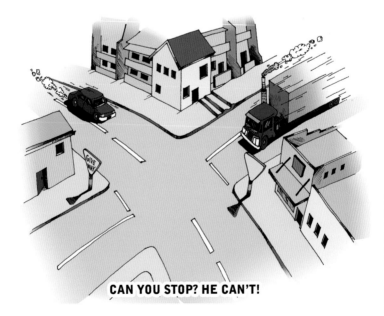

CAN YOU STOP? HE CAN'T!

RUSSIAN ROULETTE

At intersections you will see many drivers playing a motorised version of Russian roulette. Those who drive through intersections without reducing speed, always expecting that no one will cross their path, are just waiting for their number to come up.

The majority of serious crashes in built-up areas occur at controlled intersections. In all cases someone has ignored traffic signs or lights. Don't be caught by one of these people.

Danger at intersections is not necessarily created by drivers who roll through stop signs or accelerate through yellow lights.

Although they are breaking the law, these persons could be aware of the surrounding traffic. The real danger is the person who is totally unaware of the existence of signs, lights or even the intersection itself as they motor through.

Cornering

Cornering is the most difficult and most important of all these procedures. Consequently it is divided into three sections. They are vehicle position for left turns and right turns, the use of controls, and traffic check in left turns and right turns.

For safety, most intersections that do not have traffic lights use roundabouts. They are a variation of intersections and are governed by intersection procedures, but they do have a set of simple rules to follow. These rules are as follows.

ROUNDABOUT RULES

APPROACHING: Signal left for left turn; right for right turn; none for straight ahead. Vehicle position is left for left turns or straight ahead; next to centre line for right turns.

AT ROUNDABOUTS: The vehicle in the roundabout has right of way over the entering vehicle, which always approaches from the right. Only enter when clear. Be wary of the 'roundabout bully' approaching fast from the street on your right.

EXIT: Signal and exit from the left.

AT ROUNDABOUTS

Left turns are taken from the left lane – signal left.

Right turns are taken from the right lane – signal right.

Straight ahead is taken from the left lane.

If possible a left signal to exit is given at all roundabouts.

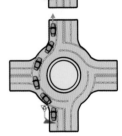

VEHICLE POSITION
(Non-roundabout)

For Left Turns

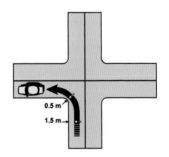

1. 20 metres before the intersection, position the vehicle approx. 1.5 metres from the kerb.
2. On turning, the vehicle moves to within 0.5 metres of the kerb.
3. The turn is completed by entering the left drivable lane.

If the vehicle is positioned too close to the kerb on approach, an incorrect wide exit must be made to prevent the rear wheel from mounting the kerb.

For Right Turns

1. 60 metres before the intersection, position the vehicle left of the centre line.
2. Commence turning when the front of the vehicle reaches the continuation of the kerb line.
3. The vehicle is turned to the right of the point where the centre lines would cross.
4. Drive to the left of the centre line in the entered road.

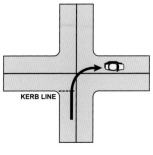

This is known as the diamond turn.

This applies to all intersections except into multi-laned roads, where a deeper turn point is needed.

USE OF CONTROLS (All corners)

In manual vehicles 2nd gear is used for left and right turns. It gives a slow approach and good acceleration out of corners and eliminates the need to differentiate between 2nd and 3rd gear corners. All gear changes are completed *before* the corner.

In automatic vehicles the gear change points are not needed.

The control use sequence is:

1. Check mirrors (SEE WHOLE SCENE)
2. Signal (BE SEEN). Give all signals 60 metres or two light poles before the corner (EARLY DECISION)
3. Position vehicle next to centre line for right turns, 1.5 metres from the kerb for left turns
4. Brake – stop lights on (BE SEEN)
5. Select 3rd gear (if in 4th gear)
6. Brake to slow (HAVE AN ESCAPE)
7. Select 2nd gear – this change is made while braking
8. Check for traffic (EYES ON THE MOVE, SEE WHOLE SCENE)
9. Complete turn – brake released, accelerator applied

2 Procedures

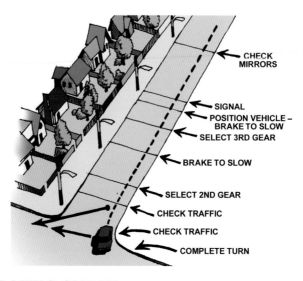

CHECK MIRRORS

SIGNAL
POSITION VEHICLE –
BRAKE TO SLOW
SELECT 3RD GEAR

BRAKE TO SLOW

SELECT 2ND GEAR

CHECK TRAFFIC

CHECK TRAFFIC

COMPLETE TURN

TRAFFIC CHECK

LEFT TURNS

1. *Preliminary traffic check:* 15 metres from the corner start checking to the right
2. *Position vehicle:* the turn is commenced well before the kerb line is reached
3. *Final traffic check:*
   a. Right: look down the road (as far as possible) before entering
   b. Left: there may be a vehicle or person in front

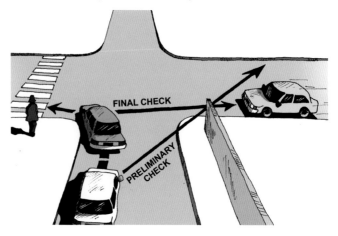

FINAL CHECK

PRELIMINARY CHECK

Left turns are more difficult than right turns because the vehicle must be turned left while the traffic is checked right. The exit line is also tighter.

RIGHT TURNS

1. *Preliminary traffic check left*: 10 metres from the corner check left
2. *Check right*: look down the road (as far as possible)
3. *Final traffic check left*: look down the road (as far as possible)
4. *Final traffic check right*: while turning look right down the road

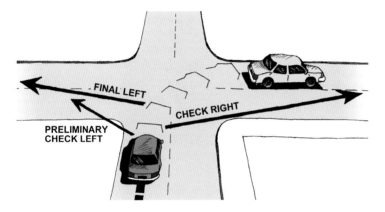

When turning right don't be preoccupied with the left traffic check at the expense of the right. The first collision path is from the right.

- During the approach to intersections, attention is always on the oncoming traffic. Its movements and rights are blended into the procedure.
- For a correct traffic check, look down every road *as far as possible*. Be aware of possible block-outs (see p. 49).
- Do not watch vehicles, watch drivers. Make **eye contact**. If they see you they won't collide with you.
- The footbrake must stay on until the final traffic check is made.

The **point of decision** is reached only after you are certain that no collision is possible, then the accelerator is applied.

- At intersections, when waiting to make a right turn or to proceed straight ahead, look continually from one direction to the other. It is only the checks both ways, *just before* moving, that are relevant.
- When checking for traffic, if needed, lean forward in the seat to improve vision. This also eliminates blind spots created by windscreen pillars.
- Because other vehicles are obliged by law or directed by sign or traffic light to give way is not sufficient reason to proceed. You must be positive, irrespective of circumstances, that there is no possibility of a collision before proceeding.
- On steep downhill corners the brake may be applied earlier. On uphill corners 1st gear may be selected to prevent stalling. On these occasions the vehicle is driven slowly up to the corner.
- Blind corners or busy intersections may require 1st gear selection or a stop.

SAFETY WHEEL IN ACTION

In the cornering procedure we witness the Safety Wheel in action:

- Correct vision habits are used (SEE THE WHOLE SCENE, AIM HIGH, EYES ON THE MOVE).
- A SAFETY CUSHION is developed.
- All the voluntary cornering decisions are EARLY DECISIONS. With the signals (both stop and directional) and eye contact, we will BE SEEN.
- Through an early decision, being seen and the safety cushion we HAVE AN ESCAPE.

This linkage will continue through all our future driving.

BLOCK-OUTS

A block-out occurs when an object – a truck, bus, tree, building road works, etc. – obstructs our vision. You may have noticed these during the cornering procedure.

The rule to follow is never proceed unless all possible collision paths are clearly visible. If forward movement is essential, it must be at the slowest speed, with all thoughts towards stopping.

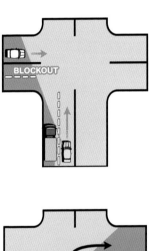

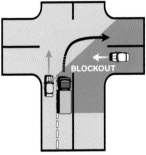

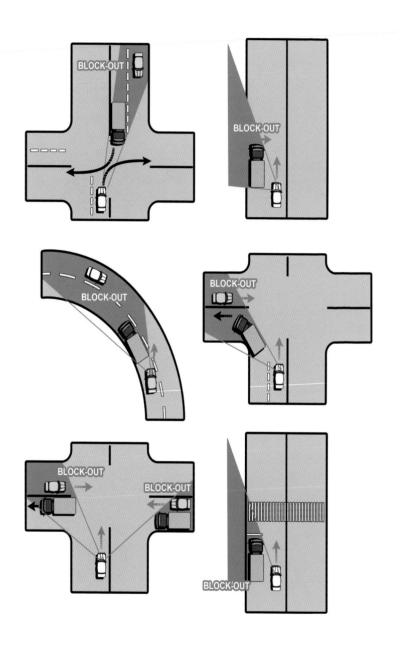

Supplement

PRACTICE ENVIRONMENT

Level suburban blocks with left and right turns with minimum through traffic. A hill is required.

CONDITIONS

Day or night. Preferably not a wet night.

LAWS AND REGULATIONS

A full knowledge is needed of the laws relating to:

LEAVING KERB	What procedures are required? What precautions are needed?
ROUNDABOUTS	Who must give way? What signals are required?
TURNS	What signals are required? How is the vehicle positioned? Who must give way?
U-TURNS	Where are they prohibited? Who must give way?
FOOTPATHS	What are the procedures before crossing? What are the pedestrian rights?
ROAD LINES	What does an unbroken line mean? What does a broken line mean? Where may you cross unbroken lines?

DO YOU KNOW?

When the brakes are applied their action is to reduce the turning of the wheels. It is this reduced turning, combined with tyre adhesion, that stops the vehicle. If the braking pressure is excessive the wheels will lock, skidding will occur and stopping efficiency will be dramatically reduced.

Brakes stop the wheels, tyres stop the car.

STOPPING DISTANCES

These are minimum stopping distances and include both reaction and braking distances. Wet roads or poor tyres can double these distances.

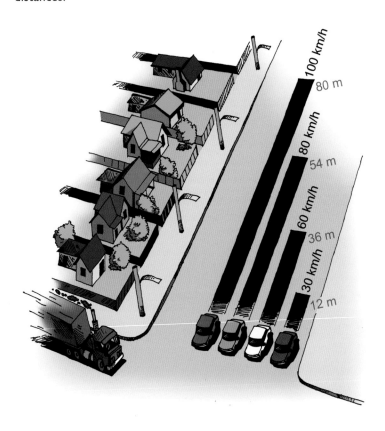

COMMON FAULTS AND MISCONCEPTIONS

LOOKING AT CONTROLS: At this stage there is a tendency to look at the pedals and gear lever. Resist this from the earliest stages – it can become a habit and is dangerous.

POOR VEHICLE POSITION: During this section, driving too far to the left or in the centre of the road is common. Develop a clear understanding of the normal drive path that exists on all roads – observe other vehicles and use commonsense.

APPROACH TO CORNERS: During the cornering procedure there can be a tendency to reduce speed early and excessively on the approach to corners. This results in incorrect pedal sequence and because of the slow approach following traffic is obstructed. Drive up to the corners, brake to slow the vehicle and arrive at the corner during the braking process.

CHECKING AT INTERSECTIONS: Traffic checks at intersections are often deficient. Look to the visible end of the road. Remember we are looking for vehicles that could collide with us and they could be travelling very fast. If waiting at intersections, keep looking to the left and the right.

ABILITY REQUIREMENTS
Do you have:

	YES	NO
A knowledge of EARLY DECISION, BE SEEN and HAVE AN ESCAPE?	☐	☐
An ability to perform the full leaving and returning to kerb procedures?	☐	☐
The ability to move the vehicle slowly forward?	☐	☐
The vehicle control to start on hills, both up and down?	☐	☐
The ability to perform U-turns correctly?	☐	☐
A clear understanding of HAVE AN ESCAPE at intersections?	☐	☐
The ability to perform the full cornering procedure adequately?	☐	☐
An understanding of block-outs and the procedure to follow when blocked out?	☐	☐
The habit of making eye contact with other drivers?	☐	☐
A habit of checking your tyres and cleaning your windows and mirrors daily?	☐	☐

3 Initial Traffic

Before attempting this section a degree of proficiency in the preceding sections is needed. Major attention must now be directed outside the car, not on the controls inside.

In this section we will concentrate on familiarisation with the general traffic situation. Specific instruction will be on *hills and bends, vision review, safety cushion development, be seen in traffic, use of controls in traffic, traffic lights, laned roads, pedestrian crossings and road signs*.

HILLS AND BENDS

Hills have a marked effect on a vehicle's performance, while bends require a different steering approach than intersections, particularly if hand over hand steering has been used.

- Select a suburban road that has hills and bends. In this exercise attempt to maintain constant speed irrespective of the terrain.
- Here gravity plays a major part in the car's performance. It is like riding a bike: effort is needed up the hills and none down.
- As you slow on the hill, increase acceleration or if in a manual vehicle change down in the gears to maintain speed.
- In manual vehicles, try to anticipate the gear change points.
- As the vehicle accelerates down the hill use the footbrake to reduce speed.

When driving uphill in a manual vehicle practise this skill:

At very slow speed in 1st gear depress the clutch; the vehicle will stop; then apply the accelerator and raise the clutch and start moving without rolling back.

Because of the reduced wheel turn needed, hand over hand steering is not suitable on bends – this is where pull push steering can be developed and used.

Vision Review

Before we drive on the main roads we will re-examine the vision points as they would apply in heavy traffic.

Park the vehicle on a main road, with good vision depth and various traffic situations visible: traffic lights, pedestrian crossing, parked cars, people, etc.

SEE THE WHOLE SCENE

- Examine the whole scene from footpath to footpath and to the visible end of the road.
- Note entering streets, traffic lights, pedestrian crossings, etc.
- The whole scene will include parked vehicles, pedestrians, cyclists, animals, light poles, trees and vehicles travelling in all directions. It also includes traffic from the rear.
- The road surface is part of the whole scene, but only for detecting hazards, potholes, debris, etc. It is not the major point of attention.
- The whole scene is continually changing.

EYES ON THE MOVE

- Keep your eyes moving from one object to another. Don't become transfixed by any one thing.
- The reason for keeping the eyes on the move is to be *aware of potential hazards – we are looking for trouble*.
- What are the potential hazards in the scene around?

AIM HIGH

- When you first examine a new scene, look to the end and see the whole scene, then come back to the immediate situation.
- This enables a good vision lead to be established. It gives depth of vision.
- Short vision habits develop by working vision away from the vehicle. Your vision then tends to stop at the first hazard or at the vehicle immediately in front.

Initial Traffic Drive

It is now time to take the initial traffic drive. Avoid difficult or stressful situations. Stay in the left drivable lane. During this drive vision habits can be practised and familiarisation with the traffic flow will commence.

- On entering any new scene look for what is at the end of the scene (e.g. there is a T-junction at the end of the road; a long way ahead the traffic is stopped). **AIM HIGH**.
- As the scene changes develop an overview of the situation (e.g. there are three sets of traffic lights ahead; there are two cross streets in this section). **SEE THE WHOLE SCENE**.
- Pick out the immediate possible danger situations (e.g. that car is signalling, it may leave the kerb; there is a boy on a pushbike). **EYES ON THE MOVE**.

Safety Cushion Development

As the situation arises the safety cushion can be developed. A safe distance should be kept from **all** vehicles in **all** directions.

- Never drive in another vehicle's blind spot.
- In laned traffic don't drive beside other vehicles.
- Stay out of the right lane: it is the head-on-collision lane.
- If road conditions permit move wider from parked vehicles and left for oncoming vehicles.
- If a vehicle is too close behind increase the safety cushion in front to allow a more gradual stop.
- When stopped in traffic leave a car space in front for roll forward room, if danger comes from the rear.

If traffic conditions dictate that we must drive close to another vehicle, *reduce speed to suit the space that exists*.

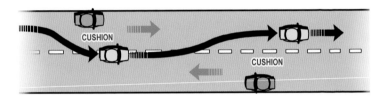

THREE-SECOND FOLLOWING RULE

A safe following distance varies with speed. To work out safe following distances with these variables would require a calculator. The problem is solved by working from another factor that is not variable: time. If time is the cushion, the following distance will automatically increase as the speed increases.

For safe driving, keep a cushion of 3 seconds between vehicles. This applies at all speeds. From the moment the leading vehicle passes a fixed object (a parked car, a light pole, etc.) 3 seconds should elapse before the following vehicle passes the same point. One easy way to calculate this period is to say, one thousand and one (1 second), one thousand and two (2 seconds), and one thousand and three (3 seconds).

This following distance should be practised until it becomes automatic at all speeds.

Be Seen in Traffic

It is important that others are aware of you. Don't drive where you are not visible to others (e.g. in blind spots, by ignoring block-outs).

Make sure others have time to see you. All movements should be commenced early and performed methodically.

The primary method of being seen is by stop and turn signals.

- By **eye contact** you know whether you have been seen. Is that driver or pedestrian looking at you?
- Attract attention, if necessary flash the headlights, tap the horn (develop a gentle tap on the horn).
- When other drivers, through courtesy or to improve traffic flow, let you through or into the traffic line, acknowledge their actions. Give them a wave or a nod in appreciation.
- Although another driver may call you on, the decision to proceed safely is entirely yours.

Use of Controls in Traffic

The proficiency gained during cornering practice should allow sufficient control to be able to drive in traffic. However, there are certain procedures that need to be explained.

INSTRUMENT CHECK

- When the traffic movement allows, check the speedo. Constant checking allows a sense of speed to develop.
- If any other warnings are displayed on the instrument panel they will then be noticed, e.g. short of fuel.

USE OF MIRRORS

- The mirrors should be checked approximately every 10 seconds.
- Use only a glance. Attention must be on the happenings ahead.
- In a *voluntary decision* situation a glance in the mirrors is always made *before* any slowing, stopping or turning manoeuvre is made.
- You need to be aware of the possible consequences to vehicles behind you of any action you take.

WAITING TO START

- When waiting in traffic, the time taken to start moving can be calculated by allowing 1 second for every car in front (2 vehicles 2 seconds; 6 vehicles 6 seconds).
- It is possible to increase vision and have an earlier warning by looking through the windows of the cars in front. This should also be practised in moving traffic.
- In the early stages, in manuals, leave the vehicle in 1st gear, with the clutch depressed. This will enable a quicker getaway. As confidence increases the car can be left in neutral with the clutch raised.
- In automatic vehicles, if there is an extended stop the vehicle may be moved to neutral and the handbrake applied.

BRAKING IN TRAFFIC

- When slowing or stopping in traffic, brake hardest early. Don't leave the hardest braking till the end.
- Gradually release the brake just before stopping to give a smooth stop.
- Leave a car length in front when stopped in traffic. This can be judged by the amount of the leading car or road visible over the bonnet (this varies for cars and drivers).
- When driving in traffic, if the right foot is not using the accelerator, keep it over the brake. This will reduce reaction time if the brake is needed.

HANDBRAKE USE

- Don't use the handbrake, unless it is needed when starting, to prevent roll back, or if the traffic is stationary for an extended period.

GEAR CHANGING

- Gears are changed so that the vehicle is in the correct gear to move forward. There is no need to change down, unless you are in 5th or 6th, if you are definitely going to stop. Stops may be made in any gear but preferably not 5th or 6th. Don't use any controls unnecessarily.

FOOT OFF CLUTCH

- Once the gear changes up to top gear have been completed, the left foot should be placed comfortably on the floor. In automatic vehicles always keep it on the floor. This is your bracing foot in the case of an emergency.

HOLDING THE CAR ON THE CLUTCH

- On hills, the car is never held by slipping the clutch and holding the vehicle at friction point. This applies maximum wear to the clutch. Use the handbrake.

Traffic Lights

STALE LIGHTS

- A stale traffic light (either red or green) is one where you are uncertain when it will change.
- In manual vehicles, when approaching a stale red light, progressively reduce the gears while braking. If the lights change you will then be in the correct gear to proceed.
- Approach stale green lights expecting a change to orange then red. This is not a time to accelerate; gradually reduce speed.

APPROACH TO LIGHTS

- Check the mirror when approaching traffic lights. The closeness of following vehicles will have a bearing on your braking.
- When approaching or crossing an intersection, attention should be on the intersecting road for the possibility of a collision.
- The yellow light means stop unless the stop cannot be made safely. Heavy, unsafe braking is not needed for a yellow light.
- The speed of approach should be governed by the visibility at the intersection.
- Slowing must continue until the *point of decision* has been reached.

AT LIGHTS

- A red light does **not** guarantee that a vehicle will not enter the intersection. Over 200,000 accidents per year occur at traffic lights in Australia. In most cases somebody disobeyed the signal.
- Don't forget pedestrians. In many cases they will ignore the lights. You must still give way to them.
- When waiting at traffic lights, watch the traffic situation as well as the lights; you won't miss the light change.
- On proceeding, don't forget – someone may turn right across your path.

- Before moving, be certain that the traffic in the intersecting road is going to stop.
- The change from red on one road to green on the other is not instantaneous. There is a time lapse between changes.

When approaching lights, as in all traffic situations, the Safety Wheel can be seen in action:

- Correct vision is being constantly used while driving.
- A **SAFETY CUSHION** is in constant operation. No vehicle should be too close.
- Because of correct vision, an automatic **EARLY DECISION** for the procedure to follow is made.
- Early braking or turning signals allow others to be aware of our actions: we will **BE SEEN**.
- The safety cushion, an early decision allowing gradual braking and being seen and letting others know our actions combine to allow us to **HAVE AN ESCAPE**.

Laned Roads

- Keep wholly within the lane. Don't wander from one lane to another, don't straddle lines.
- To keep within lanes on bends, turn the steering wheel early and gradually. Imagine you are riding a bicycle and need a smooth line to keep control.
- There is a tendency to keep too far to the left in lanes. Can you feel the bump of the raised line reflectors under the vehicle? When stopped in laned traffic are you physically positioned directly behind the driver of the vehicle in front?

Vehicle placement can be governed by the relationship of the right line to the right front of the vehicle. (This is only to be used as an initial guide – vision must be quickly restored to seeing the whole scene.)

WHAT LANE SHOULD YOU DRIVE IN?

- Generally use the left drivable lane. Use the right lane only to overtake or turn right. Remember it is the head-on-collision lane.
- When turning left into multi-laned roads, use the left drivable lane. Unless clear roadway is available in the kerb lane go directly to the second lane.
- When turning right into multi-laned roads, select the right lane but as soon as possible change to the left drivable lane.
- When driving on a roadway with three drivable lanes choose the second lane. This allows a safety cushion between you and vehicles entering from the left or right.

Pedestrian Crossings

- Pedestrian crossings are to be approached with the expectation that someone will cross.
- Check the rear-vision mirror early; the vehicle behind could influence your actions at the crossing.
- Slow when approaching until the *point of decision* has been reached.
- Be wary of crossings where parked vehicles obstruct your vision. (Little children might be crossing. Look for their feet beneath the obstructing vehicle.)
- Don't overtake a vehicle stopped at a crossing. It is obvious why it is stopped.
- Wait until pedestrians are well clear, don't intimidate them. While waiting, direct vision left and right.
- The pedestrian at a crossing *always* has the right of way.
- Do you know all the types of pedestrian crossings and the procedures needed at them?

ROAD SIGNS

Road signs are divided into three categories:

Regulatory signs, which must be obeyed. Failure to comply constitutes an offence.

Warning signs, which inform of possible danger.

Advisory signs, which give general road information.

Initially the main point is to be aware of the *existence* of the sign. Then examine its function. This is part of **SEEING THE WHOLE SCENE**.

The specific points of this section can be practised as the situation arises. Keep in mind that the major aim of the preliminary traffic section is acclimatisation to the traffic flow. Do not attempt too much. Do not make it stressful.

PRACTICE TIPS

When a front seat passenger in a vehicle, *silently* evaluate the driver.

- Is a correct steering technique used?
- Would your reactions be earlier or later? If later, why?
- Does the driver have a good safety cushion and following distance?
- Does the driver make early decisions and made sure that he or she is seen?

Critical analysis of the technique and safety habits of other drivers will enable you to appreciate and understand your own driving.

Supplement

PRACTICE ENVIRONMENT

A suburban area with hills and bends. A main road approach to a shopping centre. A multi-laned main road with moderate traffic density.

CONDITIONS

Day or night. Avoid a wet night or peak-hour traffic if possible.

LAWS AND REGULATIONS

A full knowledge is required of the laws and regulations relating to:

TRAFFIC SIGNS	What are regulatory signs? What are warning signs? Do you understand all the signs?
TRAFFIC LIGHTS	What is meant by a red light? – by an orange light? – by a green light?
PEDESTRIAN CROSSINGS	What are the various types of crossings? What are the procedures at these crossings?
LANED ROADS	What procedures are followed in laned roads? What is the procedure for changing lanes? What regulations apply to driving in the right lane?
DIRECTIONAL ARROWS	What regulations apply with directional arrows on the road?
BLOCKED INTERSECTIONS	What regulations apply?
EMERGENCY VEHICLES	What must you do if you hear a siren? What are emergency vehicles?
MERGING TRAFFIC	Who must give way?
POLICE DIRECTIONS	When must they be followed?

DO YOU KNOW?

Motor vehicles have independently sprung wheels to smooth out bumps on the road. If the wheels are independent to the body, the body is independent to the wheels.

- This can be noted under hard braking, when the front of the vehicle dives down. This reduces the rear tyre grip. Under fierce acceleration the rear of the vehicle drops and the front comes up. This reduces the grip of the front tyres. Care must be taken not to use these extremes if centrifugal force (during cornering) is applied or the lightened section may lose adhesion.
- Gravity, the Earth's pull, affects the performance of vehicles. The extra effort required uphill and the reduced effort downhill is caused by gravitational pull.

COMMON FAULTS AND MISCONCEPTIONS

RIGHT LANE DRIVING: Some drivers think the right lane is the safe lane because it is furthest from troubles at the kerb. The right lane is the head-on-collision lane. Remember the SAFETY CUSHION – use the right lane only when overtaking or turning right.

SHORT VISION: There is a tendency to only look at the vehicle in front. AIM HIGH, SEE THE WHOLE SCENE – the vehicle in front will *always* be in your peripheral vision. If necessary look through the windows of the vehicle in front.

YELLOW LIGHTS: Do not use heavy braking at yellow lights; consider the following vehicles. The yellow light means stop with *safety*.

ABILITY REQUIREMENTS
Do you have:

	YES	NO
The ability to use pull push steering?	❏	❏
The ability to use constant speed on and to negotiate hills and bends?	❏	❏
A safety cushion continually in use when driving?	❏	❏
The ability to gauge a 3-second following gap? Do you use it?	❏	❏
A degree of confidence in the use of all controls in traffic?	❏	❏
A clear understanding of and procedure at stale traffic lights?	❏	❏
Sufficient control to keep centred within your lane?	❏	❏
A safe approach to pedestrian crossings and full knowledge of give-way procedures?	❏	❏

4 Secondary Traffic

During this section more complicated traffic situations will be encountered. You will be expected to be able to drive in any traffic at any time under any conditions. The following points will be examined: *influenced decisions, turns at traffic lights, lane changing, safety driving in traffic, advanced car control, overtaking, night driving, and wet-weather driving.*

Influenced Decisions

Up to this point the final responsibility for any decisions has rested with the instructing person. It is now time for you to accept responsibility for all decisions. We have examined in detail **voluntary decisions** (procedures at corners, at signs, at lights, etc.) and briefly discussed **influenced decisions**. We will now examine influenced decisions in detail.

Influenced decisions are caused by the possibility or actuality of others making **unexpected** movements. These would generally be classified as illegal, careless or stupid movements.

Influenced decisions run through the following thought and action process:

I. There is a car at that stop sign.	KEEP AN EYE ON THE SITUATION	I. Action possibly needed.
2. They are not looking this way.	EASE OFF ACCELERATOR	2. Situation developing.
3. They are starting to move.	BRAKE TO SLOW	3. Starting to happen.
4. They are coming out.	STOP	4. Happening.

**Try matching influenced-decision situations
to the actions needed.**

- The thought and the action change with the gravity of the situation. On many occasions the situation may not develop past the first or second point. On others it could possibly go directly to the fourth point. Correct vision habits and an early decision will guarantee that this process is not hurried.

- If hard braking or evasive action is needed it means that the Safety Wheel has not been used. In cases like this, if things were a little different a collision could have occurred. Good luck rather than good management governed the situation.

MIRROR USE AND INFLUENCED DECISIONS

- In **voluntary** decisions, our first action is always a mirror check.
- In **influenced** decisions, the decision is made first then the mirror is checked and rear consequences blended into our actions.

Valuable, collision-saving time could be wasted if the mirror is checked first in influenced-decision situations.

HORN READY

Once a possible influenced decision is noted it promotes a '**horn-ready**' reaction. For horn ready the hand is placed on the horn and if needed it is tapped, not blasted. We are trying to attract attention, to make eye contact, to let others know that we are present. **If they see you in time they will not run into you.** Some situations always need a horn-ready stance:

- Driving in a lane beside a lane of stopped vehicles
- Where there are many pedestrians in close proximity
- Where you have to drive close to parked vehicles
- When edging past a block-out
- When overtaking in laned traffic

This procedure is part of an **EARLY DECISION** leading to **BEING SEEN** and **HAVING AN ESCAPE**.

Turns at Traffic Lights

RIGHT TURNS

- If no vehicles are approaching from the opposite direction and the light is green, the turn may be completed *after* determining that there are no problems from traffic on the left or right.
- If there is oncoming traffic, wait at the turning point with the front wheels pointing straight ahead. (If there was a collision from the rear, you would not be forced into the path of the oncoming traffic.) Proceed when there is a break in the traffic.
- If there is no break and the lights change, the turn may be completed. There is no need for undue haste, because there is a time delay between the red light and the green light. The turn is not completed when the lights change, but when you are positive that the approaching vehicles are not going to proceed.

Pedestrian lights work in conjunction with traffic lights and pedestrians must be given the right of way. If a pedestrian crossing is in use in the direction of the turn, wait at the turning point – not at the crossing as traffic could be obstructed.

LEFT TURNS

The main consideration is that pedestrians could be crossing at the same time. Move forward to the crossing and wait. If the lights change, complete the turn.

In turns at lights, the slow moving forward technique as practised in the Procedures section (page 39) will be used.

Lane Changing

A set procedure is used for lane changing. The vehicle changing lanes must yield to traffic in other lanes.

The procedure is:

1. **Check mirrors**: If the way is not clear the change cannot be made. Remember an EARLY DECISION is needed.
2. **Signal**: Signal to the appropriate side. Give a 4-second warning to the other vehicles.
3. **Check blind spot**: This is only a quick, over-the-shoulder, final check. The initial decision to change is made from the mirror.
4. **Change lanes**: Do not commence moving until vision is directed forward. Gradually drift into the selected lane and cancel the signal. Quick steering wheel movements are not needed.

When changing lanes do not reduce speed unless necessary. This increases the degree of difficulty as the following vehicles catch up more quickly.

N.B. You have NO right of way when changing lanes.

4 Secondary Traffic

Safety Driving in Traffic

EYES ON THE MOVE

■ Keeping the EYES ON THE MOVE means that eye holding actions or situations must be mentally processed and a decision made quickly, so that vision can return to SEEING THE WHOLE SCENE. Are you making eye contact with other drivers?

SAFETY CUSHION

The SAFETY CUSHION is continually varying with the actions of other drivers. If it is diminished, re-establish it as soon as possible. If the traffic dictates that you must reduce the cushion, reduce speed accordingly.

AIM HIGH AND SEE THE WHOLE SCENE

AIMING HIGH and SEEING THE WHOLE SCENE gives time to avoid being boxed in behind parked or right-turning vehicles. If this is happening review your vision habits. By practising SEEING THE WHOLE SCENE, we know when it is safe to have a glance away from the driving situation and when to return our attention to driving.

If you have had to resort to late decisions, resulting in severe braking or abrupt turns or manoeuvres to avoid vehicles, review the Safety Wheel and find the faults that caused these situations.

HAVE AN ESCAPE

Is your speed being reduced at all intersections so that there is no possibility of a collision?

Play **'What if?'**, **'if'** being the possible unpredictable movement of other vehicles in the vicinity. Do you always HAVE AN ESCAPE in these situations?

Advanced Car Control

Three points will be discussed in this section. They are acceleration, braking and steering around bends.

ACCELERATION

During the initial stages slow acceleration and minimum gear change points have been used. The time has come to increase acceleration and explore the speed range of the gears. There may be an initial fear of acceleration but it is not dangerous, as long as the final speed reached suits the conditions.

There are various exercises to be completed in both automatic and manual vehicles. Select a wide flat road with minimum traffic.

AUTOMATIC VEHICLES

- Quickly accelerate from a standing start until 40 km/h is reached.
- Quickly accelerate from a standing start until 60 km/h is reached.
- Slowly (so that the gearbox will change upwards) accelerate to 60 km/h, release accelerator, then re-apply it, staying in top gear.
- Slowly accelerate to 50 km/h, release accelerator, then push accelerator firmly to the floor. The automatic gearbox kick-down mechanism will operate, selecting a lower, more accelerative gear.

MANUAL VEHICLES

From a standing start, still change at low change speeds but apply more accelerator between gears.

- From a standing start, accelerate hard and hold each gear longer until 3rd gear is selected.
- At 40 km/h in 3rd gear, change back to 2nd gear and accelerate hard.
- At 50 km/h in 4th gear, change back to 3rd gear and accelerate hard.

Repeat these processes until you feel comfortable with this acceleration.

BRAKING

At the same time as acceleration is practised, harder braking can be explored. Again select a wide flat road with little or no traffic.

- At 40 km/h apply the footbrake *as hard as possible*. In older vehicles this may induce wheel lock and skidding. (Hear the screech!) Probably the vehicle will pull to one side. Once skidding has commenced the braking efficiency is markedly reduced.
- From 40 km/h apply the brakes firmly and stop quickly.
- From 60 km/h apply the brakes firmly and stop quickly
- The instructing person is to ask you to stop quickly at set points (unknown to you) and from various speeds. After each stop alight and walk the stopping distance, to develop an appreciation of the distance needed – it is quite a bit more than you may think.

BEING READY

When driving place the left foot flat against the firewall (after top gear selection in manual vehicles). This is the bracing foot at the time of an emergency.

Practise applying a little weight to this foot. When any influenced decision is made, feel the left foot and at the same time concentrate on a light steering grip and relaxed arms. With this stance vehicle control can be maintained in an emergency. Constant practice will make this an automatic reaction.

STEERING AROUND BENDS

Until this stage centrifugal force has played little or no part in the cornering process. With practice and a more advanced approach to driving, a higher speed will be used on bends. You will then notice the reaction of the vehicle under centrifugal force.

This will not be a new sensation. You have been experiencing it since you first became a passenger in a car. The force that pushes you to the side of the car when cornering is centrifugal force.

THE CONSTANT ARC

At this stage, the most important factor, when cornering, is to maintain a constant arc. Any sharp or abrupt movements during the bend can be felt.

The car is off balance. At the point of abrupt movement, cornering stress is increased enormously on the vehicle. This can be felt in your body. The feeling when a constant arc is maintained is the same as when riding a bicycle. A smooth line is needed to maintain balance and control.

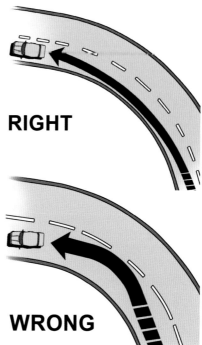

RIGHT

WRONG

Centrifugal force and the body lean of the vehicle will unbalance a driver. An effort is required to combat these forces.

- Don't lean with the vehicle.
- Keep the body balanced and the head square.

If the head leans and the eyes move from a horizontal plane, vision and perception are reduced.

The hand action needed in steering around a bend varies depending on whether the bend is slight, average or sharp.

SLIGHT BENDS

Don't move the hands from the normal steering position; just turn the wheel the required amount.

In this method on right turns, the left hand should not go past 12 o'clock; on left turns, the right hand should not go past 12 o'clock.

AVERAGE BENDS

Use the hands-ready position: before the bend the hands are placed on the wheel in a position so that when the car is in the bend the hands will be at 10 to 2. This enables the body and hands to be balanced in the bend.

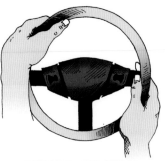

BEFORE LEFT TURN

- On left turns, before the bend, raise the left hand on the steering wheel and lower the right hand.
- On right turns, the right hand is raised and the left hand lowered.
- On entering the bend the wheel is slowly turned and the hands are at 10 to 2 throughout the bend.

To combat the turning forces, there is a tendency to lean in the direction of steering wheel turn, to take the wheel over and lean

DURING LEFT TURN

the body at the same time. This puts you off balance, reduces vision efficiency and steering control. Hands-ready steering will eliminate this practice.

SHARP BENDS

On sharp bends the pull push method of steering is used.

BOUNCE VISION

- In bends some vision is needed on the road surface, to line the car up for the bend and maintain the constant arc.
- Don't fix vision on the road surface. Bounce vision from the road to aim high, from aim high to the road, etc.
- This will enable the whole scene to remain visible.

Overtaking

In this chapter we examine overtaking in the suburban situation. Initially, practise overtaking in a narrow street where a car is parked and you must cross the centre of the road to pass or, in a wider street, practise around double-parked cars. After this, slow-moving vehicles can then be overtaken.

The procedure is:

1. *Judge distance*: Is there sufficient distance between your vehicle and the approaching traffic to complete the manoeuvre? If in doubt, don't overtake.
2. *Check mirror*: Be sure that a fast vehicle from the rear is not overtaking.
3. *Signal*: Indicate right.
4. *Select gears*: Select the gear that will give the best acceleration for the speed range.
5. *Blind spot*: Make that quick final safety check.
6. *Overtake*: Commence the manoeuvre at least 4 car lengths before the vehicle is reached. Overtake in a gradual arc; sudden steering wheel movements are not required. Quick acceleration is used to limit the time on the wrong side of the road.
7. *Return to the left*: The front of the overtaken vehicle appearing in the *central mirror* will guarantee that it is clear to move left. Signal and move left gradually.

Do not overtake through intersections or at T-junctions. Vehicles may turn into your path. When overtaking, maintain a good side safety cushion.

This manoeuvre can be practised on slow vehicles in laned traffic. A judgment of the amount of forward distance and acceleration needed can be formed without crossing the centre of the road. In lanes check the blind spot before moving back.

BEING OVERTAKEN

- If possible move to the left. This does not mean that you have to make your path difficult.
- Do not increase speed. You don't have to reduce speed unless the urgency of the situation requires it.
- Follow these practices irrespective of your opinion of the driving habits or attitude of the overtaking driver. The quicker they pass you the safer you will be.

Night Driving

The difficulties in night driving are:

- The scope of vision is reduced at night; because of this accidents increase after dark.
- Eye contact becomes difficult. Other drivers' movements become more difficult to predict.
- Pedestrians are difficult to see, particularly if they are crossing from the right and the oncoming vehicle lights are behind them.
- The lights of oncoming vehicles are a problem, particularly if they are on high beam.

Action to be taken:

- Increase the safety cushion.
- Reduce speed overall, but especially in busy or dark areas, to enable evaluation of the whole scene.
- The headlight flashing unit can be effective at night: to attract attention, to make sure we have been seen.
- Never let central vision focus on the oncoming high beam lights.

Direct central vision to the left and past the oncoming vehicle. The glare is only a real problem if central vision is directed at the lights. This can be illustrated by using a household light: central vision can be focused quite close to the globe without discomfort. Discomfort only begins when central vision is focused on the globe.

Wet-weather Driving

The problems in wet-weather driving are **reduced visibility** and *decreased adhesion*.

REDUCED VISIBILITY

- Clear visibility is reduced to the area cleaned by the windscreen wiper sweep.
- Visibility to the side and on the fringe of the windscreen is diffused. Outside mirrors become next to useless.
- Interior fogging can occur, further reducing visibility. This can be reduced by slightly lowering the windows or by turning on the demisters or the air-conditioning.
- Not only is your vision reduced but the vision of you by all other drivers is reduced.
- Pedestrians can become more interested in staying dry than in traffic movement.
- Seeing the whole scene becomes much more difficult.

DECREASED ADHESION

- Irrespective of the claims of some tyre manufacturers, no tyre adheres as well in the wet as in the dry.
- Adhesion is markedly lowered. The film of water acts as a lubricant, reducing friction and consequently adhesion.
- When cornering, centrifugal force, because of the reduced adhesion, will cause sideways sliding at a lower speed.
- The distance needed to stop is increased considerably.
- When accelerating, wheel spin can be induced.
- Wet roads are at their most dangerous after an initial fall of rain. All the grease, oil and rubber dust from passing vehicles floats to the surface and makes it particularly slippery.

Action to be taken:

- Increase the SAFETY CUSHION.
- Decrease speed because of lower adhesion and to be able to SEE THE WHOLE SCENE. Be careful at pools of water.
- Start the braking action much earlier. Pay particular attention to the vehicles behind you before braking. Reduce acceleration.
- Drive with your headlights on – others will be more aware of your presence.

THE DEADLY DOUBLE – DARKNESS AND WET WEATHER

- A disproportionate number of road crashes occur on wet nights. Under some circumstances driving can be a pleasure. This is definitely not one of them. Even the most experienced drivers find these conditions stressful.
- Visibility in all directions is dramatically reduced. Pedestrians can become almost invisible.
- Headlight efficiency drops because of light reflection.
- Speed must be reduced.
- Double your following distances. Increase the safety cushion all around.
- Drive to suit the available vision.
- Other drivers may not be following the same safety procedures.

Chauffeur Driving

Now is the time to introduce smoothness and an awareness of passenger comfort into your driving. Develop '*chauffeur driving*'.

Chauffeur driving is driving with progressive acceleration, a minimum of unnecessary lane changing and with smooth slowing and jolt-free stopping. Cornering should be without centrifugal force affecting those in the vehicle. A passenger can read a paper in the car undisturbed. Chauffeur driving should be the ideal of all drivers.

Supplement

PRACTICE ENVIRONMENT
All road and traffic conditions are to be encountered. Do not avoid dense traffic.

CONDITIONS
Day or night, wet or dry. Specific exercises should be practised during the day.

LAWS AND REGULATIONS
A full knowledge is required of the laws and regulations relating to:

PROVISIONAL LICENCES	What restrictions are placed on provisional licence holders? When must P plates be displayed?
OVERTAKING	What rules apply when overtaking? What rules apply when being overtaken?
RAILWAY CROSSINGS	What is the procedure at railway crossing lights? What is the procedure at crossings without lights?
ACCIDENTS	What must you do if you are involved in a crash?
PROCESSIONS	What rules apply to processions?
NARROW BRIDGES	What is meant by 'no passing on bridge'? What is meant by 'no overtaking on bridge'?
ONE-WAY STREETS	How do you make a right turn into a one-way traffic street? How do you make a right turn out of a one-way traffic street?

DO YOU KNOW?

The **centre of gravity** has a large bearing on a vehicle's cornering stability. High vehicles like delivery vans and some four-wheel-drive vehicles have a much higher centre of gravity than a sports car. Consequently they are more likely to roll over.

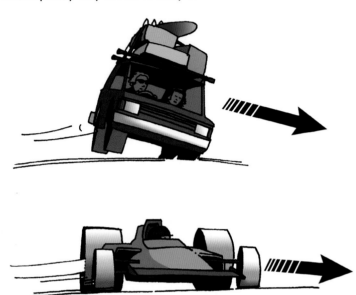

The centre of gravity can be raised in a vehicle by loading roof racks, thus reducing the cornering stability. Does your vehicle have a high centre of gravity?

COMMON FAULTS AND MISCONCEPTIONS

ACCELERATION: There may be an initial fear of more forceful acceleration. It is not the acceleration that causes danger, it is the end speed. Keep the end speed to moderate requirements.

LANE CHANGING: There is a tendency to turn the steering wheel when checking the blind spot. Make sure vision is returned to the front and you are using the side mirror before you change lane.

TURNS AT LIGHTS: If you are in the centre of the road waiting to turn right and the lights change, don't rush; you may complete the turn. There is a time lapse between light changes. Make sure oncoming traffic is stopping before you turn.

RELYING ON OTHER DRIVERS: You may have been driving for many hours without incident. Don't be misled into relying on other drivers for your safety. Safety Driving dictates that you trust only yourself.

ABILITY REQUIREMENTS
Do you have:

	YES	NO
A clear understanding of influenced decisions?	☐	☐
A knowledge of 'horn ready'? When would you use horn ready?	☐	☐
The ability to make turns at traffic lights safely?	☐	☐
Lane changing procedures correctly in use?	☐	☐
The knowledge and safety procedures to overtake safely?	☐	☐
Confidence in your ability to accelerate hard and brake firmly?	☐	☐
The ability to use the techniques needed in bend steering?	☐	☐
The ability to dispose of eye holding situations quickly?	☐	☐
The ability to re-establish the safety cushion if it is diminished?	☐	☐
Recognition of the driving line of least resistance and its use?	☐	☐
Confidence in your night-driving ability?	☐	☐
Experience in driving in wet weather during both day and night?	☐	☐

5 The Open Road

Driving can be divided into two categories – city and open road. On the open road, a much more detailed analysis of higher speed vehicle performance is needed.

In the city, cornering speed is reduced to suit the traffic situation. The cornering line follows the predestined traffic line. Speed is reduced so therefore the stress on the car is minimal.

On the open road, because of increased speed, cornering techniques and acceleration and braking performance play a greater part in safe driving.

In city driving the majority of crashes occur at intersections. On the open road single car crashes and head-on collisions predominate.

On the open road all the points of the Safety Wheel still apply.

- Vision must extend to an even greater distance.
- The safety cushion will increase because of increased speed.
- Decisions will be made earlier because of the extra stopping distance required.

Have a relaxed driving position. On the open road the time spent behind the wheel is generally longer than in the city.

There are five topics to be examined in this section:

- **Vehicle performance**
- **Open road cornering**
- **Overtaking**
- **Speed**
- **Road conditions**

Vehicle Performance

When using higher speeds on the open road, vehicle performance becomes an important factor. Many questions need to be answered.

- How quickly will your vehicle accelerate at the higher end of the scale?
- How quickly will it stop from high speed?
- What will happen to stability when braking from high speed?

ACCELERATION

Acceleration at the higher end of the speed range is very important for overtaking. Select a light traffic section of open road with width and good visibility, and practise the following:

AUTOMATIC VEHICLES

1. Accelerate smoothly at the higher end of speed range.
2. Use the kick-down mechanism to accelerate at higher speeds.

MANUAL VEHICLES

1. Accelerate in 4th gear at higher speeds.
2. Change from 4th gear to 3rd gear at higher speeds and accelerate hard.

Both of these exercises should be practised on level ground and uphill and downhill.

By noting points at the side of the road, judge the distance necessary to increase speed by 20 km/h in the higher speed range. Acceleration is noticeably decreased at higher speed.

BRAKING

From higher speed it takes a considerably longer distance and greater pedal pressure to slow or stop the vehicle.

Practise slowing and stopping from higher speed (remember 'being ready'). By noting points at the side of the road an appreciation of the distance needed to slow and stop can be gained.

CAN I BRAKE WHILE CORNERING?

Yes, if necessary, although for a correct technique braking is completed before corners.

It is quite often incorrectly stated that braking while cornering is dangerous. This is a theory from yesteryear, when brakes were unreliable and uneven in performance, and braking while cornering could affect stability. This would only apply in the modern vehicle when the limit of tyre adhesion is approached from cornering too fast. (Don't let this situation develop.)

If you need to brake when cornering, do so. Braking in corners would mostly be a continuation of the braking started before the corner.

BRAKING EFFECT OF GEARS

Using the gears to slow is not needed in modern cars. This is another practice from yesteryear. Early vehicles had unreliable brakes, which were liable to fade (not work if overheated by prolonged use). Their gearboxes had considerably lower ratios (lower change-up points). On downhill runs the vehicle would be held at a low speed by selecting a low gear.

Under normal circumstances in modern cars, with higher gear ratios, the braking effect, particularly in the higher gears, is not a helpful factor. There would only be a very slight holding action against momentum-invoked speed. On a steep downhill winding run, however, a lower gear could be the correct gear for the driving situation.

Other exceptions to this are loaded commercial vehicles, loaded family cars or vehicles used for towing. Here a much lower gear (1st or 2nd) is selected *before* a downhill slope is reached. The vehicle is held in this gear until the end of the slope.

Open Road Cornering

Increased cornering speed on the open road demands a sound technique for safety to be maintained. These paragraphs will show how to develop a technique that will apply to all corners and bends. Steering method, vision habits, road camber and the correct line for cornering are examined first.

STEERING

The steering methods for slight bends, average bends and sharp bends as explained in the Secondary Traffic section (pages 77–78) are to be used. The hands do not pass top centre of the steering wheel. Hand over hand steering is not used.

VISION

- AIM HIGH; it enables the WHOLE SCENE to be seen and an EARLY DECISION on cornering speed and line to be made.
- During the bend, vision is required on the road surface to maintain the cornering line. Bounce your vision from the road surface to aim high and from aim high to the road surface continually.
- On left turns try to see around the bend to anticipate any action needed.
- On sharp right turns it may be necessary to slightly move the head either right or left to eliminate the windscreen pillar blind spot.
- On exiting from the bend aim high as soon as possible to enable the whole scene to be visible.

ROAD CAMBER

Many roads have a camber or raised centre; this is to help drainage. Camber can play an important part when cornering.

CAMBER

- On cambered roads left turns are assisted by the camber because the vehicle leans into the curve.
- Right turns are hindered by the camber because the vehicle leans out of the curve. This creates extra body lean and places more stress on the vehicle during cornering.

Other bends may have banked turns. Mostly banking is designed to assist cornering. The banking slopes to the inside of the curve, but there are occasions where the banking slopes to the outside of the curve. This places extra stress on the vehicle during cornering.

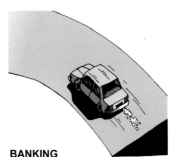

BANKING

Consequently, camber or banking must be considered when gauging the speed needed for any bend or curve. Look for different slopes on the road surface and feel the effect they have on the vehicle during cornering.

CORNERING LINE

What is a good cornering line?

A good cornering line has the effect of straightening out the bend. It reduces the stress on the vehicle during cornering.

In the illustrations, vehicle A would be more comfortable throughout the bend than vehicle B. A has a better cornering line than B.

A
RIGHT

B
WRONG

LEFT TURN LINE

- Before the bend, position the vehicle towards but left of the centre line.
- At the apex drive close to the left side of the road.
- The exit will be towards but left of the centre line.

RIGHT TURN LINE

- Before the bend, position the vehicle close to the left side of the road.
- At the apex the vehicle will be towards but left of the centre line.
- The exit will be towards the left side of the road.

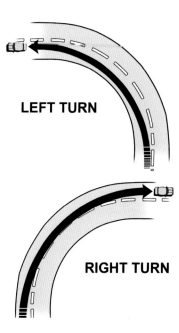

LEFT TURN

RIGHT TURN

SAFETY CUSHION

When selecting a line for a corner, don't forget your safety cushion.

- Positioning the vehicle too near the centre line means you are closer to a head-on collision, particularly if you are too wide on the exit of a left turn.

- Being too far left could place your vehicle close to broken road shoulders (quite common at the apex of left bends), roadside obstructions or parked vehicles.

- Too wide an exit from a right bend could result in your vehicle leaving the road – a common roll-over situation.

Your cornering line may have to be varied because of poor vision.

- Don't drive near the centre line at the apex of a blind right bend.
- Have a left side exit on blind left bends.

5 The Open Road

CONSTANT ARC

It is most important to have a constant arc through all bends. Steering wheel movement or a change of direction when in the bend increases dramatically the extent of the forces acting on the vehicle during cornering.

- The constant arc can be felt by the centrifugal force applied to the body during the bend. There should be no variation in this feeling throughout the bend.
- Don't use the cornering line to increase cornering speed. Use the line for vehicle control and passenger comfort.

USE OF CONTROLS IN OPEN ROAD CORNERING

To examine this topic we will divide the bend into three sections *entry, apex and exit* – and cover each separately.

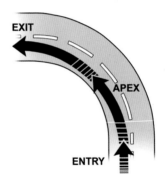

ENTRY

- Reduce speed *before* the bend. Brake early. On many occasions timely accelerator reduction is sufficient to slow the vehicle.
- Select the correct gear. This will mostly be the higher gears. Use 3rd gear on sharp or uphill bends or on steep continuously winding sections. Second could be used on hairpin bends. The gear selected is for the exit.
- Select the steering method. Start to point the vehicle into the bend well before the road turns. Correct line will allow this to be done.

APEX

- The apex is the mid-point of the turn.
- Maintain constant speed with the accelerator. If the entry was too fast or the bend downhill keep the brake applied.
- Feel the left foot on the firewall. Keep the body balanced and the head level.

EXIT

AIM HIGH, SEE THE WHOLE SCENE. Then accelerate smoothly out of the bend.

Overtaking

This is the most hazardous of all manoeuvres. On the open road, when crossing the centre line to overtake, the pulse rate of even the most experienced driver will increase.

Let us separate and examine the various components of overtaking.

ROAD LINES

UNBROKEN LINES: Never cross an unbroken line to overtake another vehicle. Obey them without question.

BROKEN LINES: Broken lines offer no information whatsoever about the safety of overtaking another vehicle. The decision rests on your perception and judgment.

PROCEDURE FOR OVERTAKING

1. Gauge the speed of the vehicle ahead; don't be too close.
2. Gauge the distance to any oncoming vehicles – remember it is almost impossible to judge their speed.
3. Check the rear-vision mirror (watch for fast vehicles from the rear).
4. Select the correct gear for good acceleration.

5. Signal (is that blind spot clear?).
6. Start overtaking at least 4 car lengths before the vehicle ahead is reached.
7. Accelerate hard, move out smoothly.
8. Tap horn if necessary.
9. Maintain side safety cushion.
10. Move slowly back to the left when the overtaken vehicle is visible in the central rear mirror. Did another vehicle follow you out and around? Leave room for it to move left.
11. Slowly let the speed settle into the normal driving range.

Ignore any signals from other drivers for you to overtake – make the decision on your judgment.

DISTANCE NEEDED

The distance needed for overtaking is variable and there is an unknown factor. What is the speed of the approaching vehicle?

Let us look at the following example, using the Sydney Harbour Bridge.

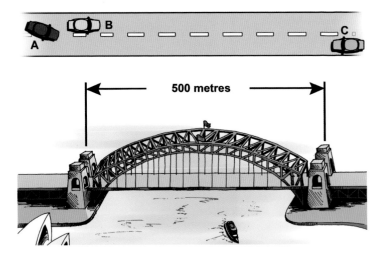

Vehicle **A** travelling at 80 km/h wishes to overtake vehicle **B** travelling at 60 km/h.

To complete the manoeuvre, vehicle **A** will be on the wrong side of the road for 8–10 seconds and will travel approximately 200 metres in this time.

Vehicle **C**, approaching from the opposite direction at 100 km/h will travel approximately 300 metres in the same time.

So the distance needed between vehicle **A** and vehicle **C** for the manoeuvre to be completed safely is over 500 metres.

This is a comparatively slow-speed example; at higher speeds much greater distances are needed.

With the assistance of your instructing person, develop the skill of judging open road distances.

THE LONG WAY AROUND

Be wary of overtaking on bends that swing to the left.

- If overtaking on a bend that curves for approximately 100 metres to the left, because you will be travelling on the wrong side of the road you will have some 10 metres further to travel than the vehicle being overtaken.
- In many cases the road camber will suit the vehicle being overtaken. The reverse camber will make the manoeuvre more difficult.
- There is the possibility of a block-out situation when passing the vehicle.

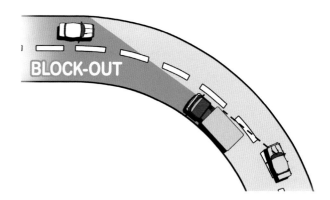

BLOCK-OUT

5 The Open Road

BEING OVERTAKEN

- Be aware of following vehicles – do not obstruct traffic.
- Give the overtaking vehicle every assistance. If they have a crash they will probably involve you.
- Don't reduce speed unless the situation demands it. The following driver has judged his overtaking on your speed.
- Don't increase speed.
- Move as far left as is comfortable. Don't move right.
- Leave sufficient room in front for the overtaking vehicle to move back to the left.

OVERTAKING HEAVY VEHICLES

- When following heavy vehicles stay well back, so that forward visibility can be maintained.
- When overtaking heavy vehicles be aware of that extra length. Be doubly sure of the overtaking manoeuvre. When halfway around it is very difficult to go back.
- Don't attempt to overtake heavy vehicles travelling in tandem.
- On narrow roads the width of heavy vehicles makes overtaking difficult. Choose a good straight stretch for the manoeuvre.
- Don't attempt to overtake on narrow road stretches if there are culverts or bridges ahead.
- Be wary of overtaking a heavy vehicle that has just crested a hill. Its acceleration down the other side could be a lot quicker than you think.

THE FINAL WORD ON OVERTAKING

If you have the *slightest* doubt *do not* overtake.

Speed

How to find **your** comfortable open road speed range:

- Are you tense?
- Is your steering grip too tight?
- Can you feel muscular tension in your arms or body?
- Are your passengers uneasy or tense?

If the answer to any of these questions is **yes**, then you are driving too fast.

Can you and a passenger hold a conversation without it being interrupted by your driving actions?

If so, this is *your* comfortable speed.

- Speed limits are the maximum speed allowed – not the expected driving speed.
- Pick your own pace – driving should not be hard work. Don't be hurried by other drivers or your passengers. You must be in control at all times.
- When cornering, choose a speed that places minimum stress on the adhesion quality of your tyres. You then have that extra adhesion as a safety zone, if an error of judgment is made.
- Until you develop a comfortable cornering speed sense, keep closely to the speeds displayed on advisory signs.
- If planning a trip, be vague with destination arrival times. Don't set time or speed goals. Just let the arrival happen.

At the other end of the scale:

- Are you meandering and obstructing following vehicles?
- Are following vehicles aggressively overtaking you?
- Are you always at the head of a queue?

If so, you are driving too slowly.

5 The Open Road

Road Conditions

Five topics will be discussed here. They are **motorways**, **paved country roads**, **road shoulders**, **gravel surfaces**, and **driving at night on the open road**.

MOTORWAYS

Motorways offer the safest form of high-speed travel. Although smashes are reduced, there are still many horrific crashes on these roads. Let us examine some of the dangers:

- Many vehicles can be in close proximity at high speed.
- There can be a vast speed difference between vehicles – as much as 100–120 km/h.
- Motorways can evoke a feeling of safety at speed, giving a false sense of security.

PRECAUTIONS TO TAKE ON MOTORWAYS

- Don't drive in the right lane unless overtaking.
- Apply the 3-second following rule, not only to the vehicle directly in front but also to the vehicles ahead in adjacent lanes.
- Remember the safety cushion; don't drive beside vehicles; stay away from groups of vehicles.
- When changing lanes be wary of fast vehicles approaching from the rear.
- Be cautious of heavy vehicles ahead, particularly on an upgrade. The speed difference could be great.
- Don't overtake on the left side unless it is absolutely necessary. Drivers are more aware of happenings on their right.

Motorways present an opportunity to practise high-speed overtaking in safety. Gauge the overtaking of slower vehicles to coincide with the movements of oncoming vehicles on the other direction of the motorway. From this an understanding of the distances needed to overtake can be formed. This exercise is invaluable – it should be compulsory and practised many times.

PAVED COUNTRY ROADS

Paved roads with one lane for traffic in each direction cover most of the country areas of Australia. Much high-speed travel and heavy vehicle movement is done on generally inadequate roads. These roads are where the majority of head-on collisions occur.

The following points are to be followed to traverse them safely:

■ Correct vision habits are essential. AIM HIGH, EYES ON THE MOVE and SEE THE WHOLE SCENE allow an EARLY DECISION to be made.
■ Develop your cornering technique. A good line and safe entry and exit for bends are needed.
■ Be aware of your vehicle's performance and stopping powers. Drive within your vehicle's capabilities.
■ Note the camber of the road and use it to your advantage.
■ Drive within your comfortable speed range.
■ Take note of all road signs and lines. Be wary of the non-advised bend or hazard. Watch for crests that are not marked with warning signs or unbroken centre lines.
■ Remember the 3-second following rule.
■ Be cautious of oncoming vehicles. Look for erratic drivers. Be watchful of oncoming heavy vehicles – at speed the wind gust of a passing truck will buffet your vehicle.
■ Animals are a hazard beside country roads. Don't assume they will stay beside the road as you pass. Often, they will panic and charge across your path. Reduce speed drastically until they are behind.

ROAD SHOULDERS

On country roads SEEING THE WHOLE SCENE includes an awareness of road shoulders. Their use is part of HAVING AN ESCAPE. If a vehicle is approaching on your side of the road you have no option but to use the shoulder.

■ If you are forced to drive onto the shoulder, be positive. Let the accelerator off and run right onto the shoulder. (Is your left foot braced?)

- Quick steering wheel movements are not needed. Don't try to force the vehicle back onto the paved surface.
- Stay on the shoulder; *gently* apply the brake. The left wheels will be on the gravel and the right wheels on the paved surface. There will be much more tyre grip on the right than on the left. Hard braking will cause the left side tyres to lose traction.
- When the speed is reduced steer positively back onto the road. Shoulders are quite often rutted next to the paved surface. Use a positive wheel turn to traverse the rut onto the paved surface.

The instructing person should select road shoulders to practise this skill at various speeds.

GRAVEL SURFACES

There are many thousands of kilometres of unpaved road surface in Australia. The reduced adhesion caused by the loose surface has a marked effect on a vehicle's stability:

- Adhesion during cornering is reduced. It is easy to induce a slide.
- Heavy braking will lock the wheels and cause the vehicle to skid on the loose surface.
- Wheel spin under acceleration is easily caused. Rear-wheel-drive vehicles will tend to sway at speed.

All these problems are increased in wet weather, when the surface is muddy. Consequently cornering is done with a minimum of centrifugal force applied to the vehicle, braking is commenced early and gentle pressure is applied to the pedal. A reduced acceleration rate and lower speeds are used.

If 100 km/h is a comfortable motorway speed, 70 km/h is a comfortable, good gravel road speed.

ONCOMING VEHICLES

When passing oncoming vehicles reduce speed and keep as far as possible to the left. Stone damage and broken windscreens occur here. When a windscreen is broken, it is not usually the thrown stone that breaks the windscreen but rather the speed at which the vehicle is driven at the stone.

DUST

Dust created by other vehicles will reduce visibility. Once again speed must be lowered. Do not attempt to overtake a vehicle that is creating a dust cloud. On these occasions visibility is reduced to nil. Be patient and, for comfortable driving, stay as much as half a kilometre or more behind the dust maker.

CULVERTS

On many occasions on gravel roads, potholes, wash-a-ways, culverts, stock grids and so on are encountered, sometimes quite suddenly and without warning:

- When they appear don't swerve or brake heavily.
- If you have time, brake gently before the hazard.
- At the hazard, slightly increase grip pressure, let both the accelerator and the brake off and keep the vehicle pointed straight ahead.
- Let the suspension cope with the bump.
- On gravel roads there are no centre lines and on many occasions no warning signs.
- On bends and curves with reduced visibility stay as far as possible to the left.
- Only overtake when visibility is excellent.
- When following other vehicles leave a 6-second gap. This will reduce stone damage to your vehicle.

DRIVING AT NIGHT ON THE OPEN ROAD

Headlights on high beam become a problem on the open road at night.

ONCOMING VEHICLES

- As soon as you think your headlights will affect an oncoming driver's vision, dip them. On straight roads this could be over a kilometre away.
- Oncoming vehicles should do the same, but many do not.

- If you think the other driver is not going to dip the lights and if he is not too close, give one short flash with the headlight flashing unit as a reminder.
- If this has no effect just suffer it out, **don't** retaliate. This driver may crash and involve you.
- Don't look at the oncoming lights; direct vision left and past the vehicle. Try to keep depth of vision. Reduce speed and move to the left.
- On right bends you will receive more headlight dazzle than on left bends. Be prepared for this.

VEHICLES AHEAD

- As soon as you can safely follow a leading vehicle, dip your headlights. Don't dazzle leading drivers by directing your lights into their rear-view mirrors.
- If a following vehicle is on high beam and close behind, a hand wave in front of your mirror may alert him.
- If the dazzle is really troublesome, slow down, let them overtake. Don't retaliate.

THE SAFE WAY

- The safest way to travel on the open road at night is to select a vehicle that is travelling at your comfortable speed and remain 100 to 200 metres behind.
- The headlights and path followed by the leading vehicle will clearly show up the bends and curves. The stop lights will warn in advance of slow sections.
- If there is trouble ahead you will be warned by the actions of the leading vehicle. Remember though, that this vehicle is only a guide. Safety Driving dictates that we only trust ourselves.
- Oncoming vehicles will dip the headlights for your pace car and stay on low beam for you.

Animals are much more active at night and are difficult to spot because of your reduced peripheral vision.

Skid Control

Sideways skidding should not be confused with straight line skidding, which is caused by excessive late braking in older cars, due to a lack of application of Safety Driving principles. Sideways skid control is a skill that, since the advent of vehicle control systems, is rarely needed and would only occur in an older vehicle. The control needed varies with the vehicle driven. These skills cannot be practised on public roadways and therefore are not available to every driver. Consequently this book does not cover the subject in detail.

Excessive momentum creating excessive centrifugal force for the adhesion qualities of the tyres causes the skid or slide. The best advice is to reduce the excessive momentum so the skid will not occur.

If you do skid, steer in the direction of the skid. When the car straightens, straighten the wheels, brake and hope for the best. Without constant practice the chances of correctly gaining control are remote. This is not a normal requisite for safe driving. If you wish to practise this procedure, it should only be done through a recognised body at an off-road facility, and after many thousands of kilometres of driving.

Supplement

PRACTICE ENVIRONMENT

All types of roadway covered in this section should be sought out. Familiar roads are more desirable. Quiet sections of road are required to practise any specific exercises.

CONDITIONS

Day and night, wet or dry. Specific exercises should be practised in daylight.

DO YOU KNOW?

CORNERING FORCES

When cornering, three forces act from the centre of gravity of the vehicle. They are:

- Momentum or forward moving energy **(A)**
- Directional control or steering **(B)**
- Centrifugal force **(C)**

Momentum **(A)** will be opposed by directional control **(B)**. By this the vehicle is directed into a circular path creating centrifugal force **(C)**. This is an outward pull.

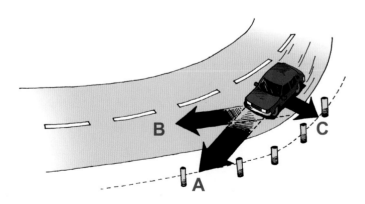

It is only the adhesion of the tyres that enables the vehicle to turn against momentum and centrifugal force. If these forces are greater than tyre grip a slide in the direction of A–C will occur; usually from the back of the vehicle, because it is the lightest part and consequently has the least adhesion.

SPEED ON WET ROADS

- At 80 km/h the tyres of a vehicle have only 7/1000th of a second to penetrate the film of water under the tyre.
- At higher speeds the tyre tends not to penetrate the film but rather to ride on the water surface. This is 'aquaplaning'.
- When a vehicle aquaplanes steering ability is lost and braking is ineffective. It is the equivalent to driving on ice. Can you think of a better reason to reduce speed?

TUNNEL VISION

- Tunnel vision occurs at speeds of over 80 km/h.
- Peripheral vision can narrow from 180° to less than 40° at 100 km/h.
- The speed smear distorts the side view. Vision shifts further ahead and awareness of side traffic is diminished.
- This is another reason why high speed in congested areas is very dangerous. You cannot see the whole scene.

VELOCITATION

- Velocitation is caused by long periods of high-speed travel. When speed is dropped, the actual speed appears to be less than it actually is.
- After travelling at 100 km/h for long periods, 60 km/h will feel like 30 km/h. Consequently the driver is not aware of the stopping distance required.
- Velocitation can be noticed when entering built-up areas after long periods of country driving. Be guided by the speedo, not the feeling of speed.
- Velocitation can be removed by completely stopping the vehicle and starting again.

HIGHWAY HYPNOSIS

This is caused by long periods of concentration while driving at high speeds. The driver is mesmerised by the surrounds. This daze could be the cause of single car crashes.

If you have been driving for some time and can't remember any passed environment or how you arrived at where you are, you could be suffering from highway hypnosis.

Stop, get out of the vehicle and have an extended break.

COMMON FAULTS AND MISCONCEPTIONS

STEERING: Hand over hand steering is not used on the open road.

LINE: There can be a tendency to commence turns too late, resulting in tight or jerked turns. After selecting the correct line start to turn before the road turns.

TENSION: Tension from high-speed travel and concentration will become evident quite early in those new to open road driving. As soon as it becomes evident, stop and have a short break.

OVER-CONFIDENCE: It takes many, many thousands of kilometres of driving to become a relaxed, expert driver on the open road.

ABILITY REQUIREMENTS
Have you had extended practice in all condition on:

	YES	NO
Higher speed vehicle performance?	❏	❏
Open road cornering?	❏	❏
Higher speed overtaking?	❏	❏
Discovering your comfortable speed?	❏	❏
Motorway driving?	❏	❏
Paved country road driving?	❏	❏
Gravel road driving?	❏	❏
Driving onto road shoulders?	❏	❏
Open road night driving?	❏	❏

6 Slow-speed Manoeuvring

This section covers slow-speed car control, using both forward and reverse gears. The techniques of close proximity manoeuvring and parking are examined.

Manoeuvring and reversing are gradually slotted into the curriculum after the Procedures section has been completed, although some reversing can be performed earlier. Manoeuvring should not be commenced until some pedal proficiency has been gained and slow moving control practised.

We will examine the following points:

- Straight reversing
- Slow-speed control
- Three point turns
- Angle parking (reversing in and out)
- Parallel reverse parking

Straight Reversing

- Use the vehicle control as practised in slow moving forward.
- Before reversing have the steering wheel in the straight-ahead position. The vehicle will then go straight back.
- Turn to the left in the seat as far as possible, while still maintaining control of the pedals and steering.
- Vision should be directed out the rear window before and during reversing. Mirrors are **only** used for reversing when there is no visibility out of the rear window.
- Steering wheel control is with the right hand on the top of the steering wheel.
- If turning is necessary, turn the steering wheel to the same side as you intend the back to go. When reversing, the vehicle is quite reactive to steering wheel turn.

Slow-speed Control

AUTOMATIC VEHICLES

Very slow starts and gentle stops are to be practised. The ability to creep the vehicle forward and backward is necessary.

MANUAL VEHICLES

Clutch control is now to be mastered. Up to this point, the speed of the vehicle has been governed by the accelerator and the brake. With clutch control the speed is governed by the clutch.

Place the vehicle facing up a very slight slope. A handbrake start will be needed. The procedure is:

1. Handbrake on, clutch in, select 1st gear, accelerator on.
2. Clutch to friction point and hold, handbrake released. The vehicle is now held stationary by the clutch.
3. Keep the accelerator on. If the clutch is raised very slightly the vehicle will creep forward. If the clutch is depressed very slightly the vehicle will slow and stop. (The clutch should not be depressed past friction point or the vehicle will roll back.)
4. It is the very slight outwards and inwards pressure on the clutch pedal that governs the speed of the vehicle. You can now move small distances with maximum control.
5. To stop, the clutch is depressed *before* the accelerator is released and brake applied.

Clutch control should not be used excessively or unnecessarily as it causes clutch wear.

Three Point Turns

Once slow-speed control has been mastered, three point turns can be commenced.

Three point turns are used to change direction in a narrow road by using forward and reverse gears. They are also an exercise in slow-speed control and reversing, which can be used in many situations.

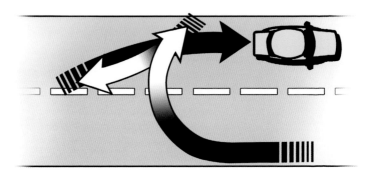

The procedure is:

1. Use normal kerb leaving procedure.
2. Use slow-speed vehicle control.
3. While moving slowly forward turn the steering wheel as quickly and as far as possible to the right.
4. Proceed as near as possible to the right kerb without touching.
5. While moving, turn the wheels halfway to the opposite lock.
6. Stop. Select reverse gear and apply the handbrake if necessary.
7. Check the roadway to the right and left.
8. Looking over the left shoulder, and turning wheels to the left, proceed back as far as necessary to be able to clear the kerb on the next forward movement.
9. Before stopping, turn the wheel halfway to the opposite lock.
10. Select 1st gear or Drive.
11. Check for traffic and proceed.

Hand over hand steering is the most efficient method for steering when manoeuvring. When manoeuvring, have the vehicle moving before turning the steering wheel. It is then considerably lighter.

Angle Parking

REVERSING IN

1. Stop with the side of the vehicle 1–1.5* metres from the parking bay and half a vehicle length past the selected parking spot.
2. Reverse straight back until the rear of the vehicle is approximately 2 metres from the selected spot.
3. Moving slowly, take the steering wheel to full lock, turning to the selected side. (Turn the steering wheel in the direction of intended travel.)
4. As soon as the vehicle is straight and parallel in the selected bay, quickly turn the wheel to the straight-ahead position.
5. Reverse back into bay.

When driving out, go at least half a car length past the bay entrance before turning the wheels.

REVERSING OUT

1. Reverse straight out for at least half a car length before turning.
2. When turning check for clearance at the front of the vehicle.
3. If the parking spot is particularly tight it may be necessary to reverse right out before turning.

When reversing straight or turning left, look over the left shoulder. When turning to the right, look over the right shoulder.

The distances quoted apply to medium-sized cars. Adjustments will need to be made for large or small cars.

6 Slow-speed Manoeuvring

Parallel Reverse Parking

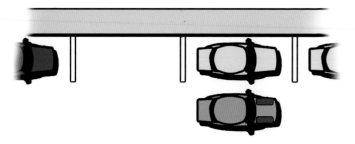

1. Position the vehicle parallel to and 1 metre from the stationary vehicle.

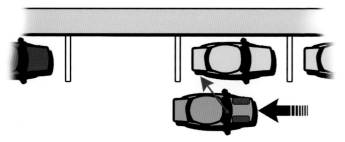

2. Select reverse, use slow-speed control and reverse to the appropriate point.*

The appropriate point will vary from vehicle to vehicle. Experimentation will determine the point in your vehicle. It is generally when the rear of the stationary vehicle is visible through the rear left window. Reversing to this point gives front clearance between your vehicle and the stationary vehicle.

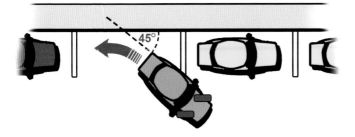

3. Moving slowly turn the steering wheel quickly to full left lock and reverse to the appropriate point.

Once again this point can vary from vehicle to vehicle:
- It may be that the kerb is just visible in the right lower corner of the rear window.
- Or the right rear corner of the stationary vehicle may be visible in the centre of the front passenger window.
- The vehicle should be 45° to the kerb.

4. Moving slowly, turn the steering wheel to full right lock and reverse until the vehicle is parallel to the kerb. If necessary, move forward and straighten the front wheels.

- When leaving the parking spot, stay on full right lock until the front is well clear of the stationary vehicle.
- When parking on hills, face the front wheels so that potential roll would be to the kerb.

Supplement

PRACTICE ENVIRONMENT

A quiet suburban area. Kerbed roads are needed, some narrow with camber.

CONDITIONS

Day or night, but preferably not a wet night. Daytime for reverse parking is desirable.

LAWS AND REGULATIONS

A full knowledge is needed of the laws and regulations relating to:

REVERSING ■ What restrictions apply when reversing?
PARKING ■ Do you know all parking restriction signs?
REGULATIONS ■ Do you know all parking restriction distances?

COMMON FAULTS AND MISCONCEPTIONS

REAR VISION: Correct rear vision is important. Many drivers are careless with vision when reversing. Look before you reverse and while reversing keep a careful watch for small children.

HANDS FOR STEERING: When straight reversing, two hands are not needed. The right hand is sufficient.

WHEN TO COMMENCE: Difficulty with manoeuvring will occur if it is commenced too early in the learning process. A delicate touch on the pedals is needed. This is only acquired after some hours of driving.

ABILITY REQUIREMENTS
Do you have:

	YES	NO
Confidence in your slow-speed control?	❏	❏
The ability to reverse straight for 20 metres?	❏	❏
The control and knowledge required to perform three point turns?	❏	❏
The ability to reverse in and out of angle parking positions?	❏	❏
The ability to parallel reverse park? (A success ratio of 3 out of 4 is needed.)	❏	❏

7 Know the Enemy

After years of experience, drivers develop the habit of identifying types of drivers that could and do cause problems. In their presence we exercise special care.

The usual way a new driver learns to recognise these types is by unpleasant or **scare experiences**. The following list attempts to identify and name the major types of potentially dangerous drivers and to give a course of action to follow when in their presence.

The list not only gives new drivers information about the potential enemy, but also serves as a reminder of what **not** to be.

CHARGER: A vehicle approaching fast from the rear. Their speed makes them a danger when in proximity to another vehicle.

- *Keep left to maintain the safety cushion. Don't become transfixed by the mirror. Keep seeing the whole scene.*

CHOKER: A road hog, a traffic obstructer, usually slow in the right lane. Drives in the centre of the road. Can block the left lane when driving beside a larger or slower vehicle.

- *Patience is required; this driver is unaware of traffic behind or beside. Overtake with caution.*

DECEIVER: Doesn't signal, signals too late or leaves signal on. Unaware of own actions.

- *Do not cross the path of a vehicle signalling, expecting the turn to be made. The driver may be a deceiver. Do not proceed until the signalling vehicle turns. Deceivers who turn right without signals are numerous.*

DITHERER: Slow to make up mind, starts then stops. Some elderly drivers are ditherers. An unpredictable driver.

- *Increase safety cushion, overtake with caution.*

DRIFTER: Inability to hold a straight line while driving. Should not have a licence. Particularly dangerous because of a lack of control.

- *Increase safety cushion. Overtake only with extreme caution.*

GROUPER: Someone who drives in a tightly clustered group of vehicles travelling in one direction. Groupers rely on the reflexes and actions of the other drivers.

- *Do not be involved. Increase your safety cushion when near groupers.*

HONKER: Unnecessarily uses the horn. An impatient driver and one who will take risks.

- *Stay aware of their presence, increase safety cushion. Let them overtake.*

INVADER: Someone who attempts to drive in your safety cushion area.

- *Move your car either left, right, forward or back to maintain the safety cushion.*

JUMPER: Leaves the kerb or changes lanes without looking or signalling. Particularly dangerous, hard to spot and a quick mover.

- *A good safety cushion at all times is the best defence.*

PACER: Drives continuously in close proximity to another vehicle, totally unaware of the safety cushion.

- *Increase your safety cushion to make up for their deficiency.*

PHONEY: A person using a mobile phone while driving; they want you to think that they are safe drivers. They are the most dangerous drivers and are regular killers: totally unpredictable.

- *Do not drive beside or particularly in front of these villains; give them a wide berth.*

POUNCER: Any person, animal or vehicle that could make an unpredictable move. Children, animals, cyclists, people alighting from cars and drivers who have not made eye contact are all potential pouncers.

- *Reduce speed. Influenced decisions procedure will apply.*

PUSHER: Drives very close to the rear of other vehicles. This individual is relying on the person in front not to brake quickly.

- *If followed by a pusher, increase your forward safety cushion to compensate for their deficiency.*

ROUNDABOUT BULLY: Approaches roundabouts at some speed, as if they always have the right of way.

- *They do not have right of way, but we are not going to tell them. Let them go, then proceed into the roundabout.*

STRADDLER: Straddles lane lines or drives to one side of a lane. Particularly dangerous on bends in laned traffic.

- *Only pass this person on straight roadway, after a warning signal and with a wide safety cushion.*

UNDERTAKER: Passes on the inside in unlaned traffic. Usually impatient and willing to take risks.

- *Slow, to allow them out of your safety cushion.*

URGER: Forces their way into your territory, mostly in slow traffic situations, at lights, in lanes and so on.

- *Allow them to proceed; maintain your safety cushion.*

8 The Complete Driver

It is the practice of this curriculum, not the reading, that will teach you how to be a safe driver.

The methods and techniques in these pages must be imprinted into your 'muscle memory', so that you will automatically react correctly, habitually and unfailingly, in any situation.

This can only happen by the correct repetitive training. This is the only way to make these skills automatic reactions. In a crisis it is the automatic reactions that will govern your fate. **Knowing how is not good enough**.

It will take many thousands of kilometres of driving to become an expert driver. During this period you will make wrong decisions and driving errors; all drivers do. As soon as an error occurs, isolate it, bring the reason for it to the surface and calmly examine it. Why did the mistake occur?

Don't let the pressure of one mistake compound into a series of more serious errors.

This self-evaluation is all part of the learning process.

If you have worked through this curriculum correctly you will be well equipped to join the legion of other drivers on the road, many of whom will not be as well equipped. You don't know any of them; they are total strangers. Don't trust them; they could be unpredictable.

Don't let pressure from other drivers or your passengers affect your decisions. You make the decisions. You and you alone are responsible for your actions. You must take the consequences of any misadventure.

There are three components to the complete driver:

VEHICLE CONTROL

The three basics of driving – starting, steering and stopping – are covered here. Cornering ability and confidence in car control are part of this section. Racing drivers exhibit the highest level of vehicle control.

One of the major errors of present thinking is that a good vehicle controller is a good driver. Good vehicle controllers, if they are lacking in the other two components, have as many if not more crashes than the average motorist. Over-confidence can often be a factor in these crashes.

SAFETY DRIVING

All the points of the Safety Wheel play an important part in being a complete driver. Correct vision and its use are prominent in this section. Although the size of big trucks may present the driver with an intimidating image, some experienced heavy vehicle drivers exhibit a high degree of Safety Driving skills. The lack of stopping power and performance of a laden vehicle means that the traffic situation must be 'read' well ahead and all actions commenced early for safe driving.

DRIVER PERSONALITY

This is you, the ever-changing you, your emotions, your temperament, your attitude.

Your attitude will vary with circumstances. You will have an entirely different view of the traffic situation if you have to travel 10 kilometres in 10 minutes, than if you have 30 minutes to travel the same distance.

If you are emotionally upset, should you drive? You cannot blame other drivers for your situation.

These individual problems have to be carefully thought through before you drive. Lowering your driving standards to suit your emotions or feelings is a short cut to a crash.

This section is the saviour of many an elderly driver. Their skill in the other two facets may have diminished, but a high level of performance in this section means that they can still drive comparatively safely. They are never in a hurry, are courteous to others and careful in their actions, and display an even temperament.

As you drive, practise your skills in these three sections.

You are the one who must meld them so that you become:

The Complete Driver